CARLISLE BAY
ANTIGUA

enjoy this beautiful book

printed for carlisle bay

ANTIGUA & BARBUDA
A Little Bit of Paradise

Edited by Arif Ali

HANSIB

This edition published in Great Britain in 2005
Hansib Publications Limited
P.O. Box 226, Hertford SG14 3WY

Email: info@hansib-books.com. Website: www.hansib-books.com

ISBN 1 870518 11 X

First edition published by Hansib, 1988
Second edition published by Hansib, 1994
Third edition published by Hansib, 1996
Fourth edition published by Hansib, 1999

Front endpaper: Nineteenth century artist's impression of English Harbour
Back endpaper: English Harbour today - photo by Joseph Jones

Design and Production by Books of Colour, Hertfordshire, England

Cover design by Graphic Resolutions, Hertfordshire, England

Printed and bound by Butler & Tanner, Somerset, England

Welcoming the world

This publication brings new illumination to any image of Antigua and Barbuda, and indeed any concept of the Caribbean, you may already have. Antigua and Barbuda is more than a little bit of paradise.

Antigua and Barbuda is an ever evolving mosaic of a region that is widely recognised as a world of its own. Nowhere else in the Antilles will you find so concentrated a mix of the essences of the Caribbean archipelago.

Antigua and Barbuda is a cosmopolitan mecca that welcomes and is enriched by people and cultures from all over the region and the world; each endeavouring, all achieving, as our national anthem affirms. Visitors will find renewal and rebirth in twin tropical islands ringed with an extravagance of superb beaches and in the spirit of a people who are uniquely spontaneous and welcoming.

Having made a decisive break with its past in 2004, Antigua and Barbuda is redefining itself as a country committed to new standards of governance as we gear up for the opportunities offered by the Caribbean Single Market and Economy and the Free Trade Area of the Americas.

We welcome the world to an ongoing celebration of the quintessential Caribbean experience and to ready access to business opportunities well beyond the Caribbean.

This publication is an engaging and authentic rendering of Antigua and Barbuda at a new dawn in the new century.

I look forward to welcoming you, as visitor and investor, to this little bit of paradise and to our two islands of opportunity.

The Honourable Baldwin Spencer
Prime Minister of Antigua and Barbuda

Prime Minister Baldwin Spencer is pictured during his official visit to Cuba in April 2005 with students from Antigua and Barbuda studying in that country

A little bit of paradise . . . revisited

It is with great pride that I invite you to enjoy this new, revised and updated version of *Antigua and Barbuda: A Little Bit of Paradise*. This revitalised publication reflects the new dynamism and vigour of our new administration elected in 2004 with a mandate to enhance our national image, stimulate business opportunities and create a balanced social environment.

A specific thrust of the Baldwin Spencer administration is the development of tourism in its various facets - the friendly and hospitable approach of our people will be harnessed in renewing our commitment to our guests, providing a quality visitor experience. This, coupled with the superior accommodation choices, excellent sailing opportunities and onshore cruise options, makes Antigua and Barbuda the ultimate destination.

The airport is our major gateway and plans are well advanced for refurbishing and modernising this facility to meet international standards at the highest level and serve as a regional hub.

We are particularly excited to host cricket patrons from around the globe in 2007 and expect to extend a welcome which is second to none. The year 2007 will also mark a number of significant anniversaries including our 40th Antigua Sailing Week and the 50th year of the greatest summer festival, Antigua Carnival.

We are inviting investors to participate in the growth of the economy and have provided a climate for easy navigation with the establishment of the Antigua and Barbuda Investment Authority. We are especially pleased to encourage our nationals living in the diaspora to make a significant contribution to the building of a new Antigua and Barbuda.

We expect that *A Little Bit of Paradise* will be situated in a prominent place in every Antiguan and Barbudan household, here and abroad, so that we as citizens can continue to appreciate this wonderful piece of heaven we call home.

A Little Bit of Paradise will be a valuable resource for every person with an interest in this country and will ignite a love and passion for its beauty through the portrayals of serene island life with a global perspective.

You will enjoy this journey through our diverse landscape, history and culture.

Minister Harold Lovell poses with US television personality, Oprah Winfrey during one of her many visits to Antigua and Barbuda

Harold Lovell
Minister of Tourism & Aviation

Hansib Publications is grateful to the following individuals, businesses and organisations for their support with this edition of *Antigua and Barbuda: A Little Bit of Paradise*:

Abbott's Jewellers
18 Heritage Quay, St John's
Tel: 462 3107/8. Fax: 462 3109
Email: abbots@candw.ag

Ace Enterprises Ltd
Airport & Factory Roads
Tel: 462 1289. Fax: 462 1290
Email: harneymo@candw.ag

Anchorage Inn
Mc Kinnons
Tel: 462 4065. Fax: 462 4066

Ambassador Ramez Hadeed
Tel: 481 2500. Fax: 462 4221
Email: hadeed@candw.ag

Ambassador David Shoul
Tel: 562 5236. Fax: 462 5238
Email: shoulamb@candw.ag

ABI Financial Group
Redcliffe Street, St John's
Tel: 480 2785. Fax: 480 2746
Email: abib@abifinancial.com

Antigua Distillery Ltd
Friars Hill Road, St John's
Tel: 480 3200. Fax: 480 3215
Email: info@antiguadistillery.com

Antigua Yacht Club Marina & Resort
Falmouth Harbour
Tel: 460 1544. Fax: 460 1444
Email: aycmarina@candw.ag

Barbuda Express
Tel: 560 7989
Website: antiguaferries.com

Beachcomber Hotel
Winthorpes Bay
Tel: 462 3100. Fax: 462 4012

Best of Books, The
Benjie's Mall
Lower Redcliffe Street, St John's
Tel: 562 3198. Fax: 462 2199
Email: bestofbooks@yahoo.com

Blue Waters Hotel
Soldiers Bay, St John's
Tel: 462 0290. Fax: 462 0293
Email: bluewaters@candw.ag

Cable and Wireless
Clare Hall, St John's
Tel: 480 4213. Fax: 480 4436
Email: info@cw.com

Caribbean Helicopters
Jolly Harbour
Tel: 562 3206. Fax: 460 5901
Email: helicopters@candw.ag

Caribbean Alliance
Long and Temple Streets, St John's
Tel: 481 2900. Fax: 481 2950
Email: gregory.manners@caribbeanalliance.com

Carlisle Bay
Old Road, St Mary's
Tel: 484 0000. Fax: 484 0001
Email: info@carlisle-bay.com

Catamaran Hotel and Marina
Falmouth Harbour
Tel: 460 1036. Fax: 460 1506

Cedar Valley Golf Club
Tel: 462 0161. Fax: 562 2762
Email: cedarvalleyg@candw.ag

Embassy of the People's Republic of China
Newgate Street, St John's
Tel: 462 1125

Colombian Emeralds International
Heritage Quay, St John's
Tel: 462 7903. Fax: 462 3351
Email: cmatthews@dutyfree.com

Cortsland Hotel
Upper Gambles
Tel/Fax: 462 1395

Crab Hole Liquors
Cobbs Cross, St Paul's
Tel: 460 1212. Fax: 460 8930
Email: crabholeliquors@candw.ag

Curtain Bluff
P.O. Box 288, St John's
Tel: 462 8400. Fax: 462 8409
Email: roberts@curtainbluff.com

Dian Bay Resort and Spa
P.O. Box 530
Tel: 480 1111. Fax: 480 1120
Email: dianbay@candw.ag

Francis Trading Agency Ltd
High Street, St John's
Tel: 462 0854. Fax: 462 0849
Email: fta@candw.ag

Global Bank of Commerce
Wood Centre
Tel: 480 2207. Fax: 462 1831
Email: bsy@gbc.ag

Governor-General's Office
Independence Avenue, St John's
Tel: 462 0003. Fax: 462 2566

Hadeed Motors
Old Parham Road
Tel: 481 2526. Fax: 481 2525
Email: hadeedmotors@yahoo.com

Harbour View Hotel
Nelson's Dockyard
Tel: 463 1026

Harney Motors Ltd
American and Factory Roads
Tel: 462 1062. Fax: 462 1024
Email: harneymo@candw.ag

Heritage Hotel
Heritage Quay, St John's
Tel: 462 2262. Fax: 462 1179
Email: heritage@candw.ag

Heritage Watches
Heritage Quay
Tel: 462 5702. Fax: 462 1006

Jumby Bay Resort
Tel: 462 6000. Fax: 562 1136
Email: pbowling@rosewoodhotels.com

Khouly Alliance Group
P.O. Box 511
Tel: 480 9000. Fax: 480 9035
Email: anicol@candw.ag

LIAT (1974) Ltd
V.C. Bird International Airport, Coolidge
Tel: 480 5630. Fax: 480 5635
Email: brownel@liatairline.com

Long Bay Resort / Inn
Long Bay Beach
Tel: 463 2005. Fax: 463 2439
Email: longbay@candw.ag

Map Shop, The
St Mary's Street, St John's
Tel: 462 3993. Fax: 462 3995
Email: cesmap@candw.ag

Ocean Inn
English Harbour
Tel: 460 1263. Fax: 463 7950
Email: oceaninn@candw.ag

Quin Farara & Co Ltd
P.O. Box 215, St John's
Tel: 462 3198. Fax: 462 3876
Email: quinfarara@candw.ag

St John's Development Corporation
Heritage Quay, St John's
Tel: 462 1078. Fax: 462 3931

Sandpiper Reef Resort
Crosbies
Tel: 462 0939. Fax: 462 1743
Email: sandpiper@candw.ag

Scotia Bank
High Street, St John's
Tel: 480 1585. Fax: 462 5463
Email: brian.murdock@scotiabank.com

Shouls Toys, Gifts and Housewares
Newgate Street, St John's
Tel: 462 1440. Fax: 462 1788
Email: shoulj@candw.ag

Sight, Sound and Time
Market Street
Tel: 462 5702. Fax: 462 1006

Stanford Financial Group Ltd
Pavilion Drive
Tel: 480 5943. Fax: 480 5922
Email: kmargetson@stanfordeagle.com

TBS Realities Inc
Crosbies
Tel: 562 7653. Fax: 560 7653
Email: tbs@tbsrealities.com

Tradewinds Hotel
Dickenson Bay
Tel: 462 1223. Fax: 462 5007

VIP (Very Initmate Places)
P.O. Box 249, St John's
Tel: 462 4065. Fax: 462 4066

West Indies Oil Company
Friars Hill Road
Tel: 462 0144. Fax: 462 0543
Email: wiocfs@candw.ag

Willowby Heights Apartments
St Philip's Village
Tel: 460 4105. Fax: 560 9738

* The international dialling code for Antigua and Barbuda is 268

Acknowledgements

***Antigua and Barbuda: A Little Bit of Paradise* could not have been produced without the help of many individuals and organisations.**

To begin with, I would like to give thanks to Antigua and Barbuda's Prime Minister, Baldwin Spencer, and his government, for commissioning this edition; to Minister Harold Lovell, who played an active role in the project from its inception and throughout; to Minister of Finance, Errol Cort for his advice; to our editorial and production team: **Managing Editor, Kash Ali**, Co-ordinator, Isha Persaud, Shareef Ali of Graphic Resolutions and Richard Painter of Print Resources and, in Antigua, Moti Persaud, Joe Antonio and Ian and Margo Marsh.

Thanks are also due to the Director General of Tourism, Shirlene Nibbs, and her deputy, Donna Cornelius, Permanent Secretary at the Ministry of Tourism, Delcine Thomas, Ursula Michael, assistant to the Minister of Tourism and the minister's secretary, Elinor Oliver, and the staff at the Ministry of Tourism; to the Prime Minister's secretary, Susan Matthias, Roy Boyke, for his continued support of the work of Hansib Publications, Ambassador Her Excellency Madame Ren Xiaoping, Bai Dongshi, Ambassador Sir David Shoul, Minister Aziz Hadeed, and the manager of the Heritage Hotel, Franklin Benjamin, and all his staff for taking such good care of me; to Brian Stuart-Young, Ian Layne, Juliene Jones and the staff at Global Bank, Rick Samuel and the staff at Antigua Commercial Bank, Eloise Green, Keva J Margetson, Sharon Ann Green, Rob Sherman at Curtain Bluff, Paul Belle, Manager of British Airways in Antigua, the staff at BWIA at Heathrow and at V.C. Bird International Airport, Cecil Wade and the staff at Amaryllis Hotel, Ella Barnes, Alan Cross, Antigua and Barbuda High Commissioner, Dr Carl Roberts, Althea Banahene and all the staff at the Antigua and Barbuda High Commission in London, Prime Minister Baldwin Spencer's Aid, 'Sheppy', Godfrey and Nicholas on gate security at the National Parks Authority, Kara Roos, for her assistance with sourcing the dive photos, UPS Translations in London, Jessica Bensley of Calabash Skyviews Ltd for the map of Antigua and Barbuda, Lucy Tullock, Michelle Franker and, of course, Pamela Mary for caring so much.

Thanks to the writers (in alphabetical order): **Sereno Benjamin**, Extension Officer working with the Agro-Tourism linkage at the Ministry of Agriculture, **Mickel Brann**, editor of *The Daily Observer*, **Mitzie L. Buckley**, lawyer, ballet teacher and owner of Siboney Publications, **Veneta Burton**, former Director of Tourism for Barbuda, **Kim Derrick**, board member and former president of the Environmental Awareness Group in Antigua and Barbuda, **Ivor Forde**, Special Advisor to the Minister of State in the Ministry of Housing, Culture and Social Transformation, **Eli Fuller**, ecologist and former Antiguan Olympian, **Sharon Green**, Sales and Marketing Manager at Antigua Distillery, **Bruce Haile Goodwin**, educator, activist and Deputy Chairman of Antigua and Barbuda's Electoral Commission, **Edward T Henry** OBE, retired Permanent Secretary at the Ministry of Education and retired curator at the Museum of Antigua and Barbuda, **Joanne C. Hillhouse**, writer of *Dancing Nude in the Moonlight*, **D. Gisele Isaac**, author of *Considering Venus* and the screenplays *The Sweetest Mango* and *No Seed*, **Colin James**, freelance journalist working for regional and international media houses, **D. Annette Michael**, Public Relations Officer at the Ministry of Tourism, **Dr Reg Murphy**, archaeologist and Director of the Nelson's Dockyard Museum, **Jan Musi**, owner of batik company Jingjok, **Dorbrene O'Marde**, Caribbean cultural worker with interests in theatre and music, **Dr Ermina Osoba**, head of the University of the West Indies Centre in Antigua and Barbuda, **Dr Eumel Samuel**, Director of the Belmont Clinic, **Martha Watkins-Gilkes**, photojournalist, environmentalist and marine conservationist, **Petra Williams**, economist and financial planner and Risk Manager for ABI Holdings Ltd.

Thanks to the photographers (in alphabetical order): **Yvonne Fisher**, Antigua and Barbuda Director of Tourism in Italy who provided many of the Tourism Department's photographs, **Ann Granger**, who operates a photo concession at Sandals Antigua, **Joseph Jones**, freelance commercial photographer, **Linton Joseph**, **Ken Maguire**, **Joseph Martin**, owner of Photogenesis, **Maurice F Merchant**, Director of Communications in the Office of the Prime Minister, **Photogenesis**, **Maurees Samuel**, **Terrance Sprague** of Photogenesis, and **David Vrancken**.

Arif Ali

Contents

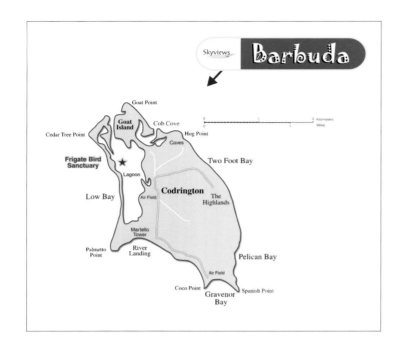

Skyviews **Barbuda**

Goat Point
Goat Island
Cob Cove
Cedar Tree Point
Hog Point
Caves
Frigate Bird Sanctuary
Two Foot Bay
Lagoon
Low Bay
Air Field
Codrington
The Highlands
Martello Tower
River Landing
Palmetto Point
Pelican Bay
Coco Point
Air Field
Spanish Point
Gravenor Bay

Map Key

	Main Road
	Secondary Road
	Other Road
	Track
	Runway
✈	Airport
✓	Customs & Immigration
Police Stn	Police Station
	Gas Station
Ⓑ	Bus Station
PO	Post Office
Sch	School
†	Church
Ⓗ	Hospital
	Traffic Light
△▽	Trigonomical Station
★	Point of Interest
	Jetty/Jetties
	Beaches

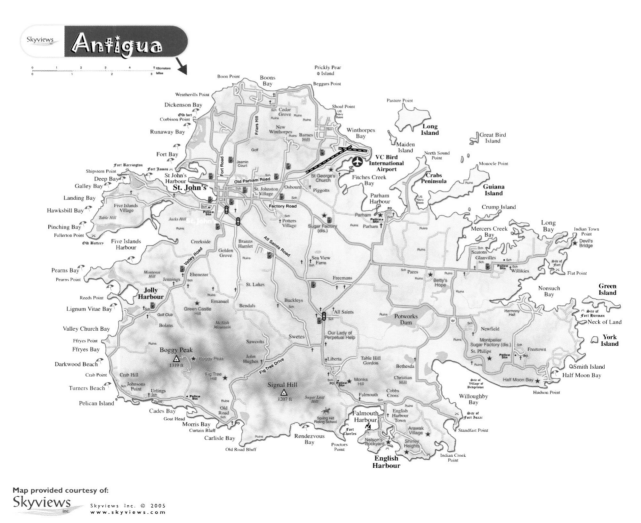

Skyviews **Antigua**

Map provided courtesy of:
Skyviews
Inc
Skyviews Inc. © 2005
www.skyviews.com

Foreword

During our first meeting, following his election victory in 2004, Antigua and Barbuda's Prime Minister, Baldwin Spencer, reminded me that, seven years ago, I had promised to produce a book on Antigua and Barbuda once he had won the election.

The publication of *Antigua and Barbuda: A Little Bit of Paradise* marks the fifth edition of a book that has been used for more than seventeen years to promote the twin-island state.

When the former Prime Minister, Lester Bird, commissioned the first edition in 1986, he asked for a book that can be used as a "one-stop-shop" to promote the country's tourism and investment opportunities. Nearly two decades later, this fifth edition is a testament to the success of this unique document and its name – A Little Bit of Paradise – has become synonymous with Antigua and Barbuda throughout the world.

Minister of Tourism, Harold Lovell is aware that Antigua and Barbuda is one of the finest tourist destinations in the world. With its 365 beaches (one for every day of the year), its friendly and welcoming population and its high standard of accommodations, he also realises that continued development and promotion will maintain the country's reputation.

This book provides an insight into a beautiful nation, a world-class Caribbean destination and a little bit of paradise.

Arif Ali
Heritage Hotel, Antigua
May 2005

National symbols

THE NATIONAL COAT OF ARMS

The Pineapple on top of the heraldic helmet represents the famous Antigua black pineapple. The Red Hibiscus flowers are symbolic of the many varieties of this plant found in abundance on the islands. The Shield with the Golden Sun and wavy blue and white bands of the National Flag symbolise the sun, sea and beaches for which Antigua and Barbuda are renowned. The Old Sugar Mill and the stem of sugar cane have historical roots and depict the cultivation of sugar cane for the production of sugar, which was Antigua's main industry. The Yucca plant or 'Spanish bayonet', with its upright stem and showy edible flower cluster at its summit was the old emblem of Antigua. The deer are symbolic of the wildlife that inhabited pre-colonial Antigua and Barbuda. The scroll bears the motto of the nation, "Each endeavouring, all achieving".

THE DESIGNER OF THE COAT OF ARMS

The National Coat of Arms was designed by Gordon Christopher with a little modification by the Statehood Celebrations Committee, 1966. Mr Christopher was born in Antigua and emigrated to Canada in 1967.

THE MOTTO OF THE NATION

The motto of the nation is, "Each endeavouring, all achieving". It was composed by James H Carrott MBE in 1967 when he was Permanent Secretary in the Ministry of Trade, Production and Labour. According to Mr Carrott, "The concept was to provide inspiration to each Antiguan and Barbudan to recognise that the development of the whole country would be a benefit to all, but that development required the effort of each individual."

THE NATIONAL FLAG

The golden sun image symbolises the dawn of a new era; red symbolises the dynamism of the people; blue represents hope; black symbolises the soil and the nation's African heritage; gold, blue and white represent Antigua's natural tourist attractions - sun, sea and sand; and the 'v' shape symbolises 'victory'.

DESIGNER OF THE FLAG

The flag of Antigua and Barbuda was designed in 1967 when the country became a State in Association with Britain. Its designer, Reginald Samuel, is an Antiguan artist, sculptor, painter and art teacher. His design was selected from among 600 entries.

The national anthem

Welcome to Antigua and Barbuda

D. Gisele Isaac

Of Antigua and Barbuda's small, interconnected society it used to be said, "If you go back far enough, *everybody*'s related." And today, the relatives have returned for a grand reunion, as brown faces from the Dominican Republic mix with those of the traditional Black, white and Arab population.

Way back when, searching for economic opportunity, our grandfathers and their brothers journeyed to Santo Domingo to cut sugarcane. Many were never heard from again, until their offspring came home to claim their birthright. And so, in the primary school classrooms, Davis sits ahead of Diaz, and Pena and Peters are best friends.

At Saturday market, Antiguan women buy vegetables from Dominican vendors; walk uptown to shop in Lebanese and Syrian stores; then flock to Spanish salons for their Sunday-morning hairdo, before picking up a take-away dinner of Chinese chicken chop suey or Jamaican jerk pork.

Light years ahead of the integration movement, this 170-square mile, twin-island nation is, without fanfare, a multi-national, multi-ethnic, multi-racial community.

Numbered among the new immigrants – the Spanish, Chinese, Africans, Guyanese and Jamaicans – are hundreds of white Americans and Europeans, who now outnumber the native-born descendants of Portuguese and Scottish merchants. Some came, like Columbus, on voyages of discovery, but decided to drop anchor – often in the picturesque seafaring communities of English Harbour/ Falmouth/Cobbs Cross in the southeast and, increasingly, Jolly Harbour in the southwest.

The burgeoning population has spread out across the island, creating communities where canefields and cow pastures once stood. The abandoned windmills – all that remains of the defunct sugar estates – are testament to the decline of agriculture and the rise of other, less labour-intensive industries, like banking, insurance, telecommunications and aviation, which have helped to build a solid middle-class.

In 1983, Antigua and Barbuda took the lead in the Eastern Caribbean to established diplomatic relations with the People's Republic of China. The two countries have since enjoyed very friendly relations, offering support to each other in the international arena. Over the years, China has provided a total of RMB (Yuan) 330 million of assistance which has funded many construction projects including the Multi-Purpose Culture and Exhibition Centre, YASCO Sports Centre, the Greekside Bridge, and highway improvement at Darkwood. Under a new co-operative agreement, China will fund and build a new cricket stadium for Antigua and Barbuda which will be completed in time for the 2007 Cricket World Cup. It is expected that the good relations between the two countries, based on equality and mutual benefit, will continue to grow and will bring more tangible benefits to the peoples of both countries.

Tourism, however, remains Antigua and Barbuda's main industry, and its many hotels – from the exclusive Curtain Bluff and the world-renowned Sandals to the locally operated Jolly Beach Resort (the country's largest property) and the VIP (very intimate places) inns – cater to every class of visitor. Cooled by tropical breezes, the sun-drenched islands are home to some of the world's most spectacular beaches – 365 white-sand treasures on Antigua and pristine, pink-sand getaways on Barbuda. The sister-island also boasts an environmentally sound lagoon that is home to a well-preserved sanctuary for frigate birds and a population of fallow deer.

With an international airport that services major carriers like American Airlines, Air Canada, British Airways and Virgin Atlantic, plus Caribbean airlines such as BWIA, LIAT and Caribbean Star, travel into and out of Antigua and Barbuda is easy and direct. And for the commercial traveller, advanced telecommunications – including broadband Internet and direct-dial international telephone – and conference facilities, make doing business almost a holiday.

Cruise-ship passengers, meanwhile, make the most of their stopovers by shopping in the capital's duty-free port; dining at the many excellent restaurants; exploring historic sites like the ruins at Fort Shirley and Nelson's Dockyard, a restored Georgian museum and boatyard; horseback riding; swimming with stingrays in the Atlantic; or kayaking around the northeast coastline.

As locals have become more affluent, leisure activities have increased and diversified. However, certain pastimes remain

14

almost sacred. Antiguans and Barbudans abroad plan their visits home in July and August to coincide with Carnival, billed as "the Caribbean's greatest summer festival," and, over eleven days, Antigua revels in a celebration of colourful masquerade, energising steelband music, sweet and/or satirical calypso anthems, and cathartic street dances that sweep away differences of race, creed and class.

For Barbuda's similarly structured carnival, Caribana, held earlier in the year, Antiguans decamp to the sister-island for a weekend flavoured with choice lobster, crab, conch, and venison.

Air arrivals are probably greatest in April, when Test cricket and Sailing Week generally take place. Cricket at the history-making Antigua Recreation Grounds is, itself, a festival where winning and losing are merely incidental to the day-long parties at which libation, food, laughter and music flow. It is here that the famous Antiguan hospitality and friendliness are most evident, as the fans who return year after year will testify.

Meanwhile, Sailing Week - one of the world's premiere regattas - attracts 'yachties' and boating enthusiasts from across the globe, transforming English, Falmouth and Jolly Harbours into hives of fevered activity. The spring Boat Show, during which the world's most luxurious vessels are on exhibition in Falmouth Harbour, is quite an experience for those buying and those looking on in wonder.

"Homecoming," the latest festival, was introduced at Independence 2004. The celebration centred on community pride, national institutions and icons, and significant historical events. As well, it featured entertainment that included zonal beauty pageants, a GospelFest, and a gala banquet and dance. Based on its success, it is expected to become an annual event.

Antiguans and Barbudans are traditionally Christian, and no matter how late into the morning the Saturday night party runs, church attendance on Sunday is generally robust. While the Anglican Cathedral of St John's dominates the city, the Methodist, Moravian, Catholic, Adventist, Baptist, Wesleyan, Lutheran and Pentecostal churches peacefully co-exist with smaller congregations like the Baha'i, Muslims and Hindus.

Apart from being the keepers of souls, the churches also play a part in keeping the culture. The Anglican and Moravian Food Fairs, for instance, are national events at which the culinary arts are equal parts exhibition and consumption. It is here that the immigrant communities come into their own, offering treats as varied as Japanese sushi, Dominican mountain chicken, Montserratian kiddie stew, and sarsaparilla, an aphrodisiac, from the Kittitians. And, of course, local favourites like souse and rice (blood) pudding; fungie and shad; and doucana and saltfish have a very short shelf life.

These events are not just church fundraisers; they are very real self-affirmations, reassurances that, despite the encroachment of North American values, cable television and the Internet, we are still West Indians where it counts — at stomach, at heart, and in spirit.

Half Moon Bay

English Harbour

Nelson's Dockyard

Barbuda

Redcliffe Quay

St John's Cathedral

A Granger

J Jones

St John's

Coconut vendors in St John's are overlooked by the statue of the 'Father of the Nation', V.C. Bird Snr

St John's Cathedral

The Lagoon, Barbuda

Half Moon Bay

Half Moon Bay

English Harbour

Photo courtesy Antigua and Barbuda Tourism Department

Photo opposite: J Jones

R Murphy

Jolly Harbour

Five Islands Harbour

St John's Cathedral dominates the capital's skyline

The distinctive rock formation at the appropriately-named Hawksbill Bay

J Jones

45

J Jones

St John's harbour

Photo courtesy Antigua and Barbuda Tourism Department

47

History built on sugar

Edward T Henry

Antigua and Barbuda was colonised specifically as a mercantile resource for the production of sugar. No serious attempts at colonisation took place until 1632 when a party of Englishmen, under the leadership of Edward Warner, set out from nearby St Kitts and landed on the southern side of Antigua and claimed it for the English Crown. They established a tenuous settlement where they lived in a state of perpetual crisis. They were under attack from the Caribs and were caught up in the wars between the English, French and Dutch as well as in the feuds of the Restoration.

The early settlers cultivated cash crops such as tobacco, indigo, cotton and ginger for export and subsistence crops for themselves. In succeeding years, sugar came into prominence. Its production shaped Antigua's landscape to this day when vast areas of rainforest were cleared to make way for sugarcane fields. During the seventeenth century, Antigua was one of the most heavily wooded islands in the Eastern Caribbean and its trees were felled to supply timber and spares for ships. Lignum vitae and other useful plants – which are now largely extinct - then flourished. The island boasted two small rivers, one at Carlisle and the other at Blubber Valley.

In 1674, a dramatic change in the island's economy took place when the first large-scale sugar plantation was established by Sir Christopher Codrington who came from Barbados. He named his estate Betty's Hope after his daughter. His success encouraged others to turn to sugar production. More than 150 sugar mills dotted the countryside, many of which are still standing today. The early planters christened many of their large estates with names that are familiar in Antigua today: Byam, Duers, Gunthorpes, Lucas, Parry, Vernon, Cochran and Winthorpe.

In 1710, Governor Park was killed in a stand off between his own militia and the planters of the day. In 1728,

there was a minor slave uprising and in 1736, a major slave rebellion was alleged to have been uncovered. The three ring-leaders - Court, Tomboy and Hercules - were 'broken' on the wheel and some eighty others brutally executed.

In 1834, slavery in Antigua and Barbuda was abolished but slaves were not 'free' in the real sense of the word; and Antiguans were still scarred from the colonial experience. Emancipation further perpetuated the hierarchy of colour and race that the British had established at the beginning of the colonial period. Stringent Acts were passed to ensure that the planters had a constant supply of labour.

The Assembly voted in June 1846 to import Portuguese workers from Madeira and the Cape Verde Islands. About 2000 arrived between 1847 and 1856, mostly from Madeira. They were brought to the island to replace the workers who left the sugar estates in order to gain recruitment in the West India army. In the early 1900s, ethnic diversity increased with the arrival of itinerant traders or 'peddlers' who came from Lebanon.

When, in early 1918, the planters decided to change the method by which cane was paid for at the factory, the result was the riot of 9 March 1918. During the disturbances, many people were killed or injured, but the planters' decision on cane payment was reversed.

Nineteenth century impression of slaves cutting cane on an Antiguan sugar estate

The founding of the Antigua Trades and Labour Union on the instigation of Sir Walter Citrine, a member of the Moyne Commission that visited the West Indies in 1938/9, marked a significant step in the development of labour relations between the planters of the day and the labourers. Most of the workers lost no time in becoming members of the trade union and, for the first time in over one hundred years, workers could be assured that their rights were protected. Among other things, the Antigua Trades and Labour Union, with its President Reginald Stevens, initiated bargaining processes with the planters and under the dynamic leadership of Vere Cornwall Bird, who succeeded him, made even greater strides in having the rights of the workers respected. The struggle for the recognition of the rights of the workers was a long and bitter one.

The opening of US military bases in 1941 placed the United States at the centre of Antigua's economic and social life but sugar remained the dominant, although declining, sector of the economy throughout the 1940s and 1950s.

The Antigua Labour Party (ALP), with its trade union base, fought and won all subsequent elections, save one when the Progressive Labour Movement (PLM) won in 1971 and George Walter became Premier. But the ALP was again returned to power in 1976. Under the Bird administration, Antigua achieved independence in association with Great Britain in 1967, and full independence in 1981. In March 2004, the Antigua Labour Party was defeated at the polls for only the second time in its history. The United Progressive Party (UPP), under the leadership of Baldwin Spencer, won the elections and formed the Government.

Nineteenth century impression of barrels of sugar being loaded into rowing boats for transfer to ships anchored in Willoughby Bay

A DEPENDANT SISTER ISLAND

With a population of around 1500 people, Barbuda is a relatively flat island of limestone formation lying approximately thirty miles north of Antigua. Its highest point is a mere 128 feet in an area known as The Highlands. The island boasts one of the finest beaches in the Caribbean which is located at Coco Point.

Barbuda has had a long history of dependence, first as a private leasehold of the Codrington family (1685-1870), then as a Crown colony and later as a dependency of Antigua. For many years, the political relationship between Antigua and Barbuda has been an uneasy one but with the recent success of the United Progressive Party at the polls, bold steps have been taken to improve this situation and a member of the Barbuda Council (which was formed in 1977) now sits as a member of the Cabinet of Antigua and Barbuda.

When Barbuda became a part of the new state of Antigua and Barbuda in 1981, its natural endowments were disrupted. It was clear that its small-scale productive economy that, in the previous century, relied on the salvage of ship wrecks, fishing, hunting and farming, could not continue to support the needs of a growing population. Many people emigrated but kept in touch with the homeland, making remittances to their families from time to time.

Over the past three decades, its natural resources, particularly its beaches, have become vulnerable to commercial exploitation. Sadly, Barbuda has benefited fractionally from the vast revenues drawn from the sand mining industry over the years and its environment is now in danger of being seriously impaired. The many coral reefs that surround the island make it dangerous for shipping, but provide a haven for fishing and scuba diving. And, on land, it offers a hunter's paradise with and abundance of wild boar, deer, guinea fowl, pigeons and ducks.

Nineteenth century impression of the Gracehill Estate in Antigua

Preserving national treasures

Reg Murphy

Photos: R Murphy

English Harbour, in the Parish of St Paul, has a long and colourful history. It was first settled approximately 4000 years ago by Archaic Age fisher/forager peoples. They were a nomadic, marine-oriented culture that utilised the marine and terrestrial resources of the area. These peoples are believed to have originated from South America, migrating north through the islands in small groups. Evidence of their occupation has been found by archaeologists on the seafront near to Clarence House, and the mangrove flats near to Cobbs Cross.

During the middle of the first millennium BC, they were displaced by pottery-making, Arawak people from the lower Orinoco region of South America. The Arawaks introduced many of the edible and useful plants to Antigua that are still used today. These include cotton, tobacco, papaya, guava, pineapple, cassava and corn. They established large settlements at Indian Creek, Mamora Bay, Freeman's Bay, Rendezvous Bay to name a few. The Arawaks were to occupy Antigua until the arrival of the European explorers in 1493. By the time of English settlement in 1632, the native peoples - dubbed 'Caribs' by the Europeans - had abandoned Antigua and Barbuda.

However, the rich marine resources of the island was essential to their survival and resistance against the English colonists continued sporadically for another fifty years.

Although it is debatable exactly which European was the first to settle in Antigua, credit is generally attributed to Edward Warner for his successful colonisation of the island. Members of the Warner family themselves in the Piccadilly area, and the tombs in their private cemetery, although badly vandalised, can still be seen today. Archaeological investigations are currently in progress at this site to gain insights into the life and times of this little-known period of Antigua's history - the early years before sugar and slavery.

During these early years, Falmouth was established as a place of commerce and settlement and English Harbour as a safe harbour for shelter and repair of ships. Further development saw the establishment of the British Naval facilities - the Antigua Dockyard, now called the Nelson's Dockyard – followed by the numerous army barracks built on Shirley Heights. Throughout this period, everything was built using the labour of African slaves.

With political recognition of the importance and values

The dockyard capstan is pictured in the foreground with HMS Rose in the background

Archaeology student excavating an Arawak village site

Stones from the original sea wall which was built by slaves between 1815 and 1820

of the south-eastern coast of Antigua, the Nelson's Dockyard National Park was established in 1984. The National Parks Authority (NPA) was established by Act of Parliament to manage, conserve, protect and develop the rich cultural, historical, archaeological and natural resources of the area. Covering approximately eleven square miles (about ten percent of Antigua), the park begins at Mamora Bay and ends at Carlisle Bay. The demarcation line follows the ridges of the coastal highlands or watershed. After an initial lengthy public consultation process, the area was zoned, with each area designated for specific types of development. These include tourism, residential community, conservation and natural habitat zones. This policy serves to guide and ensure the sustainable development of the area and stands as a successful model that should be applied to the rest of the island.

To implement its mandate, the National Parks generates revenue through user fees - admission, rental of restored buildings, and management of its resources such as the marina and hotel. The dockyard is viewed as a continuing cultural landscape and strives to maintain a balance of historical authenticity within a 21st century technological environment.

One of its strongest yet least-known sectors of the National Park is its research and archaeology program. The Dockyard Museum and Field Research Centre host annual field schools with the University of Calgary and many interns, graduates and researchers visit annually to work under the supervision of the museum and archaeology director. This joint program continues to add new and tangible insights into the history and material culture of the islands and the surrounding areas.

The Nelson's Dockyard National Park, the gem of St Paul's, is one of the leading heritage tourism attractions in the Eastern Caribbean. The beautiful landscapes, and the rich history and seafaring culture, contribute significantly to the economy of Antigua and Barbuda today, and it will continue to do so for many generations to come.

Nelson's Dockyard

English Harbour is one of the safest anchorages in the Caribbean. With its natural deep water, flanked by protective hills rising to over 450 feet, it was developed by the British Navy as a dockyard in the middle of the 18th century. Later named Nelson's Dockyard in honour of its most famous resident, Britain's Admiral Horatio Nelson, the dockyard stands in tribute to the 'age of sail'. As one of the finest remaining Georgian naval facilities of its day, the dockyard continues to function as a facility dedicated to the service and accommodation of seafarers and their vessels. It is the historical core of the National Parks of Antigua and Barbuda, a protected area and the premiere heritage tourism destination in Antigua. The historical structures and naval facilities have been recently restored and upgraded to the best international standards, and with its many fine restaurants, boutiques, museums, nature trails and handicrafts, Nelson's Dockyard has become a unique, world class heritage site.

Sea wall reconstruction

Bullet shells and cannon balls excavated in 2002

The roots of a vibrant culture

Dorbrene O'Marde

Antiguans and Barbudans practice and exhibit a culture that reflects attributes from their African ancestry and heritage, the historical effects of British colonialism and the recent North American economic and political influences in the Caribbean region. The national culture is further informed by the physical factors of extremely small geographic size, relatively flat topography and tropical climate The synthesis of these influences – historical, biological, physical and psychological - has also yielded an emerging philosophy and cultural expressions that are, without doubt, uniquely Caribbean.

The range of cultural activities and experiences available in Antigua and Barbuda has broadened in the last twenty years through the influx of Caribbean peoples from other islands, notably Jamaica, Guyana, Dominica, the Dominican Republic and Montserrat. In addition, there has been growth in the Lebanese, Syrian, Asian, North American and European segments of the population but these migrants are more active in the economic life of the country than its popular culture.

The nature of the dominant cultural traits and those performing and visuals arts which depict the national culture, is African. The official language of the country is English but most Antiguans speak an English dialect that is sprinkled with African linguistic retentions and speech patterns. The steelband and calypso rhythms find roots in the centrality of the drum to African music and culture, and popular dance is

A trip across the Lagoon in Barbuda

Nelson's Dockyard

J Jones

J Jones

A Granger

made distinct by the preference for motion in the waist and the hips of dancers.

Antigua has witnessed, like many other Caribbean countries, a phenomenal rise in the popularity and political power of the new Christian 'religious right' that continues to challenge the traditional dominance of the established churches. Popular religious thought, however, still acknowledges the active existence of a spirit world and in Antigua there are remnants of the practice of *obeah*, an African based system of spiritual beliefs.

Traditionally, the Christmas period was the highlight of cultural creativity and production in the country. However, the Antigua Carnival, staged annually during the summer period (July/August) has, since its inception in 1957, replaced the Christmas period and associated festivities as the cultural focus. It is at that time of year and in a joint celebration of emancipation from slavery and summer tourism that Antiguans are at their creative best. It is at Carnival when composers create new music; when new dances evolve; when the graphic artists and costume and clothes designers blossom; when dramatic skills are revealed in both youth and adult pantomime and song presentation.

Antiguan musicians, in shared endeavour with other regional artists - mainly in the soca, calypso and steelband music forms, have made notable international impact in the furtherance of Caribbean culture. Soca group, the Burning Flames are presently the most popular and internationally recognised of Antigua musicians. The role of the calypso as a medium for both entertainment and socio-political development is heralded through national competitions that make national heroes of consistent winners. Sir McLean Emmanuel (The Mighty Short Shirt) was knighted by the Antiguan government for mastery of the calypso artform. Other artists such as Paul Richards (King Obstinate) and Rupert Philo (King Swallow) have been given national awards for their calypso exploits also. Reggae and dance hall music are also important local and regional forms. Steelbands such as Hells Gate, Harmonites and Gemonites continue the tradition that heralds Antiguan bands as among the finest in the region.

There is a long tradition of drama in the Antigua society developed around the natural inclination of the population towards story-telling, recitation and the '*Singing Meeting*' where practitioners of verbal arts battle each other or laud their

Sailing on the Jolly Roger is a popular tourist attraction

J Jones

J Jones

56

J Jones

linguistic mastery over awed and appreciative audiences. However, there has been a decline over the last two decades of the practice of theatre arts. Creative writing is predominantly expressed through poetry and fiction and new writers, grappling with the establishment of a literary tradition and sensibility, are emerging. There is a minor tradition of the publication of social and political study and the practice of journalism now struggles to find legitimacy in the newly found democratic environment.

The dance is once again popular. A number of dance groups such as the Antigua Modern Dance Academy, Shiva and the VS Dancers, inspired by regional and international influences and the 'dance of the street', regularly produce shows of exciting choreographed material.

Antigua, no longer a major producer of agricultural products, imports food from virtually every continent in the world. It offers a cuisine that is comparable to the finest regional and international fare. In addition, culinary artists, especially in the tourism sector, are interestingly beginning to recognise and utilise the foods and cooking methods of the native population in their creations.

Antiguans and Barbudans continue to battle the new and efficient forms of cultural penetration such as cable television and the US publishing industry with their values and value-systems that promote both social and economic dependence on products and thoughts generated externally. There is recognition in the country, however, that it is cultural uniqueness which defines and protects its national identity and confers viability on its participation in world affairs.

Dorbrene O'Marde is a Caribbean cultural worker with major interests in theatre and music

English Harbour

The pier at Codrington in Barbuda

A Granger

J Martin / Photogenesis

With its roots in West Africa, 'warri' is Antigua and Barbuda's national board game

59

Photo: J Martin / Photogenesis

Martello Tower, Barbuda

Antigua and Barbuda Defence Force

J Martin / Photogenesis

The Antigua and Barbuda Police Force celebrating 'Police Week'

J Martin / Photogenesis

Market in St John's

Photo courtesy Antigua and Barbuda Tourism Department

Tug-o-war' on the beach - a popular pastime

L Joseph

HMS Endeavour sailing into English Harbour

St John's Cathedral

Local beauty queens

Dominoes at the fire station

St John's Cathedral
Photo: J Jones

The heart and soul of the nation

83

The unsung female influence on the nation

Mickel Brann

The woman's story in patriarchal Antigua and Barbuda is more than a tale of the strong, yet silent, female behind the successful man. From Edith Richards (the first woman to seek elected office in 1956) to Dr Jacqui Quinn-Leandro (the first woman elected to Parliament in 2004) and all the success stories in between, women in the twin-island nation have good reason to feel proud.

While the representation might not be equal and the playing field far from level, young girls in modern-day Antigua and Barbuda certainly have role models to emulate.

In the field of politics, three women sit in the Upper House; Senator Gail Christian, Senator Joanne Massiah and President of the Senate, Hazelyn Francis. These women stand on the shoulders of the forerunners who were perceived, at best, as upstarts who were ahead of their time.

History will find special mention for Ruth Samuel, the first woman appointed to the Senate by the Progressive Labour Movement (PLM) administration; Senator Millicent Bailey, who was the first woman to serve at the pleasure of the Antigua Labour Party (ALP); and a sister from yesteryear, Bertha Higgins, who was appointed by the late Rt Hon. V.C. Bird Sr to the Federal Senate in 1958.

D. Gisele Isaac, who took the Speaker of the House baton from Dame Bridget Harris (the first woman to serve in that capacity), is executive secretary at the Board of Education. Kathleen Forde is the boss at Central Marketing Corporation

Dr Jacqui Quinn-Leandro

Senator
Joanne
Massiah

Queen Ivena

Photogenesis

Photogenesis

J Jones

(CMC); Dr Ermina Osoba is the chairwoman of the Board of Education; Valerie Hodge has responsibility for the National Parks Foundation; and Dr Linda Lovell-Roberts is the government's Acting Chief Medical Officer. Of the sixteen permanent secretaries, eight are women: Vincere Bachelor, Governor General's Office, Barbara Belle, Ministry of Justice and Legal Affairs, Agnita Bleau, Ministry of Information and Broadcasting, Vernessa Matthew, Ministry of Social Transformation, Enis Nathaniel, Ministry of Labour and Public Policy, Cora Richards, Prime Minister's Office, Delcine Thomas, Ministry of Tourism and Aviation, and Maudlyn Richards, Ministry of Agriculture, Lands, Marine Resources and Agro-Industries.

In business, the lore accords a handsome helping of reverence to the memory of the late Sissy Nathan, a landowner and moneylender from the 1940s. "She was powerful, a person to be reckoned with," mused historian Selvyn Walter who, as a young boy, read for the ageing Nathan. Her industriousness has helped pave the way for women like Eileen Murraine, the first woman in the Eastern Caribbean to be appointed General Manager within the Royal Bank of Canada.

The woman's story in Antigua and Barbuda would not be complete without paying homage to the merchants (who traded mostly in fabric) including Mary John, Gisele Michael and the maverick, Edris Silston, who was among the first to retail ready-made clothes.

The art sorority celebrates Higgins as the mother of the movement in Antigua and Barbuda. In the 1940s, before steelband took its pride of place, she invited members of the Hell's Gate Steel Orchestra into her living room and taught them to read and write music. Tribute must also be paid to another first lady; Director of Culture, Heather Doram, who is an artist, actress, costume designer and the creator of the national dress. And we must not forget the female calypsonians, who have razed the boys' playground in recent years, not least among them the diminutive, twice-crowned monarch, Lena "Queen Ivena" Philip. Or the women responsible for putting the country on the literary and film industry map, like Jamaica Kincaid, Joanne Hillhouse and the present Speaker of the House, who penned Antigua's first two feature-length movies, *The Sweetest Mango* and *No Seed*.

In the field of education, women are at the forefront, dating back to the era of the Spring Gardens Moravian Teachers Training College, whose principals aimed to empower women in this regard. Avis Athill, Agatha Goodwin, Mary Pigott, Nellie Robinson and Gwen Tonge, who brought respectability to home economics, are some of the educators lifted onto pedestals. And it is difficult to ignore the fact that the latest statistics show that girls are outperforming boys in the classroom.

Sportswomen, too, have hoisted Antigua and Barbuda's flag high in the international arena, namely middle and long-distance runner, Janill Williams who struck gold at the Pan American Junior Games in 2001, and Desiree Francis who, in 2000, was selected to play (albeit for one season) in the WNBA for the New York Liberty.

"Women have been the unheralded, unsung and unrecognised leaders who have helped to shape the society," Walter said. This is about much more than cigarettes and smoke, but the American slogan, "You've come a long way, baby" rings true.

Musical expression

Dorbrene E. O'Marde

The early folk music of the Antigua and Barbuda reflects the influences of African and European traditions. West African song and dance traditions were transplanted to Antigua (and the rest of the Caribbean) where they influenced, and were influenced by, the existing dominant European traditions transplanted by slavers and traders.

National specific music forms emerged in various Caribbean territories. The nature and functions of these forms were dependent on the levels of African retentions in the society and the intensity of European cultural intrusion into the thinking of the African masses. In Antigua and Barbuda the dominant form emerging from the meeting of African and European traditions was known as 'bennah'.

Bennah shares common characteristics with all the other types of African-Caribbean music. Its form was that of the litany or 'call-and-response'; its themes were dominated by praise, blame or ridicule and women were generally its main subject. The songs tended to be improvised rather than composed and musical accompaniment was by drum or other percussive instrument.

The most famous of the bennah singers during the middle of the last century was a man named John Quarkoo who sang at street corners on the 'topic-of-the-day', echoing the thinking of the masses labouring under colonial rule at the time. In typical traditional African fashion he used song to ridicule oppressors and wrong doers.

Bennah eventually came under the influence of the more developed Trinidad calypso transplanted to Antigua through

'King Obstinate'

J Jones

'Short Shirt'

J Jones

'Scorpion'

Photogenesis

'Queen Ivena'

L Joseph

J Jones

'Calypso Franko'

J Martin / Photogenesis

the early recordings and appearances of calypso troubadours like Lord Melody, Brynner and Sparrow. Today, calypso and its derivative, soca, are the main forms produced and consumed by Antiguans. Over the years, the country has produced many artists who have had international impact helping to shape and change the direction of calypso. King Obstinate (Paul Richards), King Swallow (Rupert Philo) and Short Shirt (McLean Emmanuel) are immortalised as creative pioneers. The national calypso competition, staged during the annual Carnival celebrations (July/August), has become the highlight of musical production and performance in the country. A final group of ten to twelve artists, chosen from an original field of up to one hundred singers, performs two calypsos each in a competition against each other before thousands of excited fans. The present monarch of the Antigua calypso competition is female - Queen Ivena (Ivena Phillip).

Antigua has a fine tradition of orchestras and combos which provided music for all forms of celebrations and became important to the provision of entertainment to the emerging tourist industry. The Laviscount Brass, formed in the late 1950s by John Laviscount, is still perhaps the best band in the country. It retains the name of the founder

Singing Althea

Photogenesis

Harmonites Steel Orchestra

J Martin / Photogenesis

J Jones

although he has not been associated with the group for at least four decades. Other important groups were the bands of national cultural icon Oscar Mason ('the Vibratones' and 'Sons of the Vibratones') along with the Ambrose Quintet, Gardner All Stars and the Saints Brothers. Smaller groups like the Entertainers (which featured Roland Prince who emerged as an internationally renowned jazz guitarist in the early 1970s), the Targets, Teen Stars and Playboys, provided dancing music for the youth of the 1960s and beyond. But without doubt, the most successful musical group coming out of Antigua and Barbuda is the Burning Flames, a family unit (originally) that has dominated electronic music production here since the early 1980s to this day. The group has performed around the world with its eclectic mixture of

voice, rhythm and melody capable of encouraging wild merriment and unhindered dancing.

The steelband, although introduced also from Trinidad in the 1940s, had parallel development in Antigua and Barbuda and many 'firsts' for that twentieth century musical instrument were created by Antiguans. The first steelband that was commercially recorded, Brute Force, is from Antigua. Organised/judged pan competitions, 'all-girls' steelbands, steelband associations and a number of specialised pan instruments, evolved in Antigua even before Trinidad. During the 1950s and 1960s, it is estimated that there was a steelband in every village and urban community. Among the best would have been Hells Gate Steelband (the first band formed in Antigua and probably the oldest steelband in the world), Red

Halcyon Steel Band

Army, North Star, which became Rising Sun, along with the modern bands like Supa Stars, Harmonites and Halcyon.

Steelband went through a period of decline in the late 1970s but has once more regained much of its popularity during the last decade. The pioneering stalwarts such as Eustace Manning and Fundoo Bloodman are still involved in the pan movement which is currently led by younger talented individuals such as Victor Babu Samuel, Patrick Stone Johnson and Lacu Samuel. The Gemonites Steelband has produced an annual steelband festival - 'Moods of Pan' - for the last six years featuring many regional 'pannists' and small steelbands. That festival is fast becoming internationally recognised for the quality of its musical offerings and its organisation.

After calypso, reggae music in its various manifestations is perhaps the most important music in Antigua and Barbuda. Most bands and singers will perform all genres of music but reggae is particularly popular with regional and international visitors and residents alike. Choral singing, religious music and jazz are also important musical forms. Keyboard player, Winston Bailey is today perhaps the most important musician contributing extensively to all these forms.

There is a most curious phenomenon in Antigua and Barbuda. The best of Antiguan musical talent can be experienced 'free' to the patrons in hotels, restaurants, nightclubs and casinos, where most of the better artists are employed in the service of the dominant tourism industry.

Carnival - a national tradition

J Jones

Photogenesis

Photogenesis

J Jones

J Jones

A Granger

J Martin / Photogenesis

A Granger

J Jones

A Granger

J Jones

Photogenesis

A Granger

J Jones

J Jones

J Jones

J Jones

J Jones

A unique gourmet experience

Sereno Benjamin,

When British planters were the only farmers in Antigua and Barbuda they cleared the island forest and planted sugarcane. Some people say that is the reason why crops produced in Antigua has a distinctive "it's the sugar in the land" taste.

The growing of fruit and vegetables, and the rearing of livestock, is undertaken by many small producers who market their produce through a Central Marketing Corporation. This organisation also contributes towards agricultural development and assists in the education of farmers. The organisation plays a major role in maintaining good agricultural practices on the island.

Producing food to satisfy the local demand, particularly the tourism sector, is one of the objectives of producers. Hotels and restaurants purchase locally-produced crops and livestock.

Fruits, vegetables, herbs, spices and cotton make Antigua and Barbuda's agriculture unique. Farmers learned to cultivate in the sunny, dry climate, utilising these conditions in producing the tasty treats common to Antigua and Barbuda. Farmers produce a variety of organically grown fruits, vegetables and ground provision, or rear livestock. Fruits like mango, finger rose (a type of banana), banana, sugar apple, citrus fruits, passions fruits, melons (water

Photo courtesy Antigua and Barbuda Tourism Department

THE DEFINING TASTE OF PARADISE

Rum has been produced in Antigua since the mid-1700s and was an economically successful by-product of a thriving sugar industry. Individual sugar estate owners began by producing their own varieties of rum by using old pot stills to distil their home brews. These were the first rums of Antigua.

In 1932, a group of local businesses joined together to form the Antigua Distillery Ltd. In 1934, the company purchased nine sugar estates and a small sugar factory.

Rum is made by distilling fermented sugar and water. The sugar - derived from the sugar cane - is fermented from either cane juice or molasses. Molasses is a by-product from the production of brown sugar. It is a highly sweet, sticky residue that is left after the sugar cane juice has been boiled and the crystallized sugar has been extracted.

The molasses, or cane juice, is mixed with water which is then fermented and later distilled to produce a concentration of alcohol. After distillation, the alcohol is siphoned off into oak barrels (casks) to commence the ageing process. Ageing is done in oak casks previously used for aging bourbon and, depending on the distillery or the 'recipe', can last from two years to over thirty years. Antigua Distillery, itself, proudly champions its '1981 Vintage Rum' and an 'Extra Old Rum' which are often featured in many of the region's finest restaurants. Once the ageing process has been completed, the blending process begins and then, finally, the bottling.

Today, most rums are made from molasses, but some rums in the French Caribbean islands are still made from cane juice and are referred to as 'rhum agricole'.

Rum is produced in most of the islands of the Caribbean with each island producing its own unique blends. For example, Antiguan rums are copper column-distilled and are smooth, medium-bodied with good ageing characteristics; Barbados produces light, sweetish rums from both pot and column stills; Jamaica produces aromatic rums, from light to heavy, mainly from pot stills; and Puerto Rico has light, dry rums produced from column stills.

Rum conjures up images of the Caribbean – exotic beaches, crystal-clear waters, beautiful sunsets and, of course, cocktails. With more and more varieties available, it would be impossible to name them all. However, the challenge is to sample as many as you can – either neat or as part of a cocktail – for a truly memorable taste of paradise.

Sharon Green

102

J Jones

J Jones

J Jones

melon, cantaloupe and honey dew), papaya ("pawpaw"), pomegranate are among the popular fruits. Tamarind and avocado are also grown. Gooseberry, cherries, sour-sop and plums (yellow and red) are among the fruits that are found locally.

There are many rare and little-known tropical fruits growing wild, including the 'sea grape' which, unlike grapes, do not grow on vines but on trees which are located on or near the beach. The 'gut apple' is found along streams and smells like a rose but has a bland taste. 'Macau' is a golf ball-sized fruit which grows on a palm tree but is not as plentiful as the date palm. Dates are usually available from

coconut vendors who can be seen throughout the country. The 'monkey pear' is a burgundy-coloured fruit which is produced by a vining cactus and resembles the kiwi fruit, but unlike the kiwi, the flesh is white.

The prized fruit of the country is the Antigua black pineapple, renowned over the world for its rich, sweet taste. This golden fruit is cultivated in the south of the island and has gained recognition among chefs and restaurateurs both locally and worldwide. Consequently, the government is supporting efforts to give the fruit a premium brand and offers incentives to encourage farmers to increase production.

The Palm Restaurant at Blue Waters

Photo courtesy Blue Waters

'East' at Carlisle Bay

Photo courtesy Carlisle Bay

Market days are busy and colourful with a wide variety of produce on sale. Almost every type of fruit or vegetable can be bought, including peas, corn, peppers (hot, seasoning and sweet), carrots cucumbers, cabbages, lettuce, squash, pumpkin, beets, dasheen, cassava, yams and sweet potato. The sweet potato is one of the nation's most important root crops and is used in a wide variety of recipes including 'doucouna', a dish which reflects the country's African heritage. 'Babul', which is a bread made from cassava, is one of the most popular ways in which cassava is used. And during the Christmas period, yams become plentiful.

Spices and herbs such as allspice, citronella, rosemary, chive, thyme and basil are common ingredients in Antiguan food. The 'widdy-widdy' bush, is a herb that was brought over from west Africa. Lately, the use of plants and herbs in traditional medicine is regaining momentum as an alternative source of healing. Several thriving herbal gardens can be found around the island as a result of the recognition and important role herbs and spices play in local cuisine.

Although sugarcane is not grown for export, it is still produced by farmers across the country. It is a popular crop enjoyed by locals and visitors alike. Sugarcane vendors can be seen mainly in St John's.

Another major crop which is important to the agricultural sector is West Indian sea island cotton. Antigua and Barbuda's Central Cotton Station is famous for its role in maintaining the only gene bank of all types of the sea island cotton. Sea island cotton producing countries obtain their planting materials from Antigua and Barbuda.

Cattle, sheep and goats are the major livestock and are found grazing on pasturelands or roaming across the country. Deer may also be found in Barbuda.

Fishing is another important aspect of the agricultural industry. Sea food is becoming popular as both a healthy choice as well as a delicious alternative to meat products. Lobster, conch, shrimp and a range of fish dishes are popular in the home as well as on the restaurant menus.

The blend of its culture, people, local foods and dishes set against the backdrop of the magnificent beaches and breathtaking sceneries are some of the attributes that makes this little bit of paradise a unique and unforgettable destination.

Sereno Benjamin is an Extension Officer, and has been working with the government of Antigua and Barbuda for the past 25 years. He worked with the Agro-Tourism team that was implemented to combine the departments of Agriculture and Tourism.

J Jones

TURNING UP THE HEAT

It was during the mid-1960s that Susanna Tonge decided to produce her own hot pepper sauce in order to supplement her income. With only one other business producing hot pepper sauce, she felt that her new venture would stand a good chance of survival. Her first sauces were prepared in a coal pot and cooked in the back yard. She used 'peggy-mouth' peppers that she bought from local farmers and bottled them in used ketchup bottles. Susanna branded her product as "Susie's Hot Sauce", and it soon became the nation's leading hot pepper sauce. When she passed away, her daughter, Rosie, took over the business and continued to build upon her mother's legacy. Susie's Hot Sauce now has an international presence. It has featured on the Food Network Channel and has won major awards including the Texas Shootout Challenge, widely regarded as the Academy Awards in the world of hot pepper sauce.
Mitzie Buckley

CARIB BEAN COFFEE ROASTER

On a hilltop overlooking the vista of Falmouth Harbour is the aromatic haven of Carib Bean Coffee Roaster. Coffee beans pave the walkway to a little island house set in a tropical garden which is a window to the world of specialty coffee.

Coffee is freshly roasted every day and visitors are welcomed to observe the hands-on process; from the exotic array of bags of green estate-grown Arabica coffees of the Caribbean Basin and distant lands, to the "Bean Machine" as the roaster is fondly called, and finally to the heady bouquet of the finished product.

Owners, Tim and Nora are passionate about their product, and are committed to enlightening their customers on the history and mystery of coffee and how it travelled to the islands of the Caribbean, and was introduced to the 'New World'.

Custom blending and private labelling are available for the hospitality industry. Signature house blends include 'Classic Yachtsman Blend', in honour of the Antigua Classic Yacht Regatta, 'Jump Up Java', inspired by Antigua Carnival, 'Tropical Morning Blend', for those magical island mornings, 'French Island Roast', of historical significance, 'Lava Java', to commemorate the Montserrat volcano, 'Joy in the Morning', to celebrate the dawning of a new day, 'Hurricane Brew', in memory of a few…, 'One Luv', in honour of Bob Marley, 'Journey's Blend', 'Bambu Brew' and a superb 'Primo Espresso Roast'. There is also a selection of premium decaffeinated coffees which include the popular 'Clipper Ship' and 'Espresso Decaf'.

Although available in shops and supermarkets in the area, the Java House is well worth a visit. Enjoy a 'New World' taste sensation and wake up to the aroma of freshly roasted coffee in true Caribbean style. As they say at Carib Bean Coffee Roaster, "Put a little island in your cup."

Local fruit vendor 'Fitz', right

CRAB HOLE LIQUORS

Crab Hole Liquors is one of the major wholesale and retail businesses in Antigua and Barbuda. Located at Cobbs Cross in Antigua, the company sells a wide variety of liquors from around the world. This enterprising business is managed by Leslie Roberts (pictured), one of a small handful of women in this field.

Over the last ten years, Crab Hole Liquors has grown from a single retail liquor store to a major, nationwide enterprise. It is now a household name in Antigua and Barbuda as well as in neighbouring Caribbean islands.

Committed to giving back to the community, Crab Hole Liquors is one of the major sponsors of social events and community activities, and is the sole sponsor of the Revo Band, St Paul's Cricket Club, Golden Eye Calypso Tent and the four times winners of the 'Band of the Year' at Carnival, Revellers Mas Camp.

Betty's Hope was built in 1674 by Sir Christopher Codrington. The site was one of the first full-scale sugar plantations in Antigua

J Jones

The 'Pillars of Hercules' are situated at the entrance to English Harbour

J Jones

Catholic church of Our Lady of Perpetual Help in Tyrell's

'Hell's Gate'

Jumby Bay

Falmouth Harbour

Johnson Point

NELSON'S DOCKYARD

Situated in the south-east of Antigua, Nelson's Dockyard, along with the surrounding Shirley Heights and Monks Hill, comprise the most scenic and historically attractive part of the island. Named after England's naval hero, Admiral Horatio Nelson, the dockyard has become one of the most popular sites in Antigua for tourists and yachtsmen alike.

Construction of the dockyard was initiated in 1725 by Captain Arthur Delgarno of HMS Southsea Castle, who reported to the Royal Navy that "English Harbour might be made a very proper place for careening and refitting, and so save HMS ships the trouble of going to northern colonies for that purpose". His report was accepted and supported by the Antigua Legislature which purchased twenty acres of land and presented them to the Admiralty.

Construction of a careening wharf began on the eastern side of the harbour and a fort was built to replace the small battery that guarded the entrance. Within three years the first dockyard, then called St Helena, was in use. Further development of the site continued throughout most of the 18th century.

English Harbour gained prominence after Britain lost the American colonies following the American Revolution (1775-1783), with activity at the harbour reaching a peak during the Napoleonic Wars (1800-1815).

At more than 275 years old, the harbour has become a thriving yacht basin which has undergone careful renovations and development to maintain and enhance its historic value. Every year, the dockyard plays host to sailing regattas and boat shows which have gained international recognition. *E.T. Henry*

Nelson's bedchamber

J Martin / Photogenesis

Photo courtesy Antigua and Barbuda Tourism Department

Photo courtesy Antigua and Barbuda Tourism Department

Photo courtesy Antigua and Barbuda Tourism Department

HMS Endeavour visiting Nelson's Dockyard

T Sprague / Photogenesis

Photo opposite: J Jones

St John's - a vibrant island capital

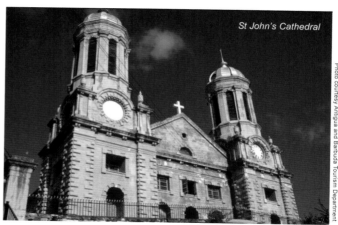

St John's Cathedral

St John's Cathedral

J Jones

J Jones

J Martin / Photogenesis

St John's

Barbuda - an exclusive tropical paradise

Veneta Burton

Barbuda is the sister island of Antigua and lies 28 miles to the north. It is 62 square miles or about fourteen miles by eight miles in size with a population of approximately 1500. The island is, largely, flat - with a high point of 125 ft - and is one of the few remaining unspoilt islands in the Caribbean. Barbuda can be reached in fifteen minutes by air or one hour and thirty minutes by ferry service from Antigua.

The original inhabitants were the Arawaks and the Caribs and they called it Wa'Omoni, meaning "land of the herons". After 1493, the Spanish named the island "Barbuda" because of its 'bearded' appearance due to its forested landscape. It is said that in 1628, settlers from St Kitts called it "Dulcina" because of its pleasantness.

Codrington is the only village on Barbuda and was named after Christopher Codrington who, in 1685, leased the island for 185 years. The boundaries of Codrington were set by the British town and country planners. They experimented with the idea of planning a city by dividing living spaces into rectangles. To the west, the lagoon marked one boundary; the north by Sedge Garden; the east by Indigo; and the south by the Park. Barbuda's historical sites include Martello Tower (or River Fort) which is a lookout post that was built to defend the main anchorage. Another historical site is Highland House, although it is known locally as "Willybob". The Codrington family built the house sometime after 1720 on the highlands of Barbuda.

The world's largest nesting colony of the magnificent frigate bird is located in Barbuda. The island is also home to several caves and sink holes including Bryant, Darby, Indian and Dark cave. It is within these caves that visitors may view ancient petroglyphs (rock carvings) made by the island's earliest inhabitants, the Amerindians.

Barbuda is well-known for its shipwrecks, and with more than 147 sites are dotted around the island, it is a scuba-diver's paradise. With some of the world's most exclusive hotels, including Coco Point and K-Club, the island is a favourite holiday destination for film stars, royalty and world leaders. With its spectacular seventeen miles of unbroken, pink coral sand beach, Barbuda truly is a little bit of paradise.

A Granger

A Granger

J Martin / Photogenesis

Photo courtesy Antigua and Barbuda Tourism Department

Photogenesis

J Martin / Photogenesis

Martello Tower

125

The splendour of the natural world

Kim Derrick

Blessed by year-round warm weather, the strong easterly Trade Winds, and a fairly well defined wet and dry season, Antigua and Barbuda sits on the north-easterly tip of the Caribbean archipelago. Antigua's average yearly temperature is 27°C, and during a normal year, the island receives about 45 inches of rainfall.

Antigua roughly divides into three distinct topographic regions: the volcanic south, the central plains and the north-eastern coral-limestone region. Barbuda is mainly characterised by sand dunes and limestone. Most of Antigua and Barbuda's land area is covered by dry savannah. On Antigua, the shrub-like mesquite (*prosopis juliflora*) and *acacia* dominate the landscape. Barbuda still possesses much of its original dry forest with white cedar (*tabebuia pallida*) predominating and large grassland areas of mostly Seymour grass (*dichanthium aristatum*)

Fringing coral reefs and rich mangrove areas surround much of both islands and provide important nurseries for many fish and shellfish species. Antigua and Barbuda has almost twice as many acres of mangrove as the rest of the English-speaking Lesser Antillean islands combined. Because they sit on the largest fishing bank in the Eastern Caribbean - the Barbuda Bank - Antigua and Barbuda is known for its exceptional sports fishing.

Mangrove areas provide excellent platforms for bird watching and learning about ecosystems. Barbuda's

J Jones

Nesting brown pelicans

E Fuller

Pond lillies

J Jones

J Jones

Pond lillies

J Jones

J Jones

Codrington Lagoon is home to the most significant population of magnificent frigate birds (*fregata magnificens*) in the western hemisphere. Thousands of these majestic birds return to perform dramatic nesting rituals in the lagoon's isolated mangrove stands every year. The McKinnons Pond, on the outskirts of St John's, transforms into a second home for numerous bird species between March and June. Species like the black necked stilt – which has the largest leg to body ratio of any bird after the flamingo – and white-cheeked pintail ducks (*anas bahamensis*), various herons, egrets, sandpipers and warblers can be spotted wading in the mudflats.

On the uninhabited North Sound islands, glimpse relictual stands of the flora most closely resembling what Christopher Columbus would have encountered during his 15th century visits. Because of their coral reefs, sea grass beds and mangrove, small fry literally jump out of the water when boats slice through the waves. This area is perhaps the jewel in the crown of Antigua's environmental assets. Here, the critically endangered Antigua racer snake (*alsophis antiguae*), West Indian whistling duck (*dendrocygna arborea*), hawksbill (*eretmochelys imbricata*) and green turtles (*chelonia mydas*) all make their home.

In the 17th century, fallow deer (*dama dama*) were introduced for hunting on the North Sound's Guiana Island and have survived until today due to the keen

Deer on Guiana Island

Common moorhen

Green back heron

stewardship of the island. While boating there, if you are quiet, you may glimpse these shy animals during early morning or late evening.

The North Sound islands are also home to innumerable seabirds. Brown pelicans (*pelecanus occidentalis*), brown boobies (*sula leucogaster*), red-tailed tropic birds (*phaethon aethereus*) with their attractive tail streamers, American oystercatchers (*haematopus palliates*) and several varieties of terns as well as the ever-present seagull, all compete for nesting sites on these tiny islands. If you're lucky you might see an osprey (*pandion haliaetus*) or two.

Although much of Antigua was deforested by the early 1700s for sugar cane cultivation, many native plants still exist. Most of the island's evergreen deciduous forest remains on the southern peaks. A few southern valleys like the Wallings watershed, next to the scenic Fig Tree Drive, contain notable moist forest species. A nature hike along the Wallings' trails promises breathtaking coastal views and glimpses of lush flora such as a wild iris (*trimezia martinicensis*) several orchid and bromeliad species, the majestic kapok or silk cotton (*ceiba pentandra*), the curious, bearded ficus spp and the enormous fan-shaped leaf of

Allamander or 'golden trumpet'

J Martin / Photogenesis

Brown pelican

A Granger

Photo courtesy Antigua and Barbuda Tourism Department

E Fuller

the leather-coat tree (*coccoloba pubescens*), a relative of the sea side grape. While hiking, listen for the shrill cries of the broad-winged hawk (*buteo platypterus*).

The black, lesser Antillean bullfinch (*loxigilla noctis*), with his red throat, and the yellow-breasted banaquit (*coereba flaveola*) which has black upper parts and sports a white stripe above the eye, are two of the islands' most common birds. Also often sighted are the zenaida dove (*zenaida aurita*), the ground dove (*Columbina passerina*) and several species of hummingbird. Visitors may be surprised to see the introduced European house sparrow while in St John's.

When touring the island, you may glimpse the Indian mongoose (*herpestes auropunctatus*) scurrying for cover in roadside bushes. Since its 1870s introduction, the mongoose has reproduced to the detriment of many egg-laying species. In spite of this menace, ground and tree lizard populations abound on the islands, as do three types of gecko. The introduced marine toad (*bufo marinus*) has also become a pest species and can be seen throughout the islands. In contrast, two tiny tree frogs (*eleuthrodactylus johnstonei* and *E. martinensis*) are rarely seen but are heard every evening performing one of nature's greatest symphonies.

Adult and juvenile frigate birds. The red-breasted male is in mating ritual

Male frigate bird in mating ritual

J Jones

Egret

E Fuller

T Sprague / Photogenesis

E Fuller

131

West Indian whistling duck

A Granger

J Jones

A Granger

M Watkins Gilkes

Hermit crab

Tree frogs

A LAND OF HIDDEN TREASURES

It may be one of the world's favourite Caribbean tourism destinations, but the twin-island nation of Antigua and Barbuda is also a nature-lover's paradise.

Antigua is home to the highest concentration of nesting hawksbill turtles in the Caribbean. Around fifty of these endangered sea turtles lay their eggs on a small beach at Jumby Bay — also the location of one of the Caribbean's most exclusive resorts. The Jumby Bay Hawksbill Conservation Project was established in 1987 under the aegis of the Wider Caribbean Sea Turtle Conservation Network (WIDECAST). It is the world's longest-running tagging project for hawksbill turtles.

An array of nesting birds - some endangered - are found on the uninhabited off-shore islands of Great Bird, Little Bird, Lobster, Hell's Gate, Red Head, Rabbit and Exchange, all located off the northern coast of Antigua. Depending on the time of year, many species of birds inhabit these islands including the endangered West Indian whistling duck, ospreys, falcons, frigates, tropic birds, turns, noddies and laughing gulls.

One of the world's rarest snakes may also be found here. The Antiguan racer (alsophis antiguae) is a gentle and harmless grey-brown snake which was saved from extinction in the early 1990s.

The Caribbean experience would not be complete without the ubiquitous sound of the tree frog. This rarely visible, thumbnail-sized frog begins its chirping at around sunset or after a rain shower.

Along with its beautiful pink-sand beaches, Barbuda is home to the world's second largest colony of magnificent frigate birds (Fregata magnificens), with an estimated population of around four thousand. Antigua's sister island is also home to the Barbuda warbler (Dendroica subita), a species of bird found nowhere else. *Martha Watkins Gilkes*

Flying gurnard

Angelfish

Four-eyed butterfly fish

LIFE BENEATH THE WAVES

Around much of Antigua, the surf breaks on barrier reefs which are teeming with marine life. It is acknowledged that there are at least 1000 square miles of coral reef surrounding Antigua and Barbuda.

Cades Reef is one of the more well-known and stretches for more than two miles along the leeward coast of the island. Part of it has been designated as an underwater marine park and is popular with locals and tourists alike. Life beneath the surface is abundant with hundreds of species of fish swimming amid the staghorn coral that flourishes throughout the shallow reefs.

In the seas around nearby Barbuda, the crystal clear waters are a sub-aqua paradise. As well as the ubiquitous coral reefs and marine life, the seabed is littered with ancient shipwrecks, mainly on the Atlantic side. However, most are not easy to locate or even identify because they are overgrown with coral.

While the beautiful white sand beaches that surround both islands provide a tropical paradise for sun-worshippers, there is a completely different kind of paradise to be discovered beneath the waves around Antigua and Barbuda. *Martha Watkins Gilkes*

D Vrancken

Sea Turtle

M Watkins Gilkes

Octopus

D Vrancken

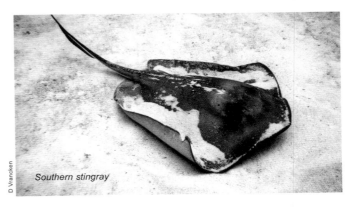

D Vrancken

Southern stingray

M Watkins Gilkes

Caribbean lobster

D Vrancken

The nation's education system

Ermina Osoba

The education system in Antigua and Barbuda, a legacy of British colonialism, is basically structured along the lines of the British system. It is a three-tier system of primary, secondary and tertiary institutions. The first primary schools were established by various Christian denominations, particularly the Anglicans and the Moravians. Women have also played a critical role in the development of education in Antigua and Barbuda. Mention must be made of pioneers such as Nellie Robinson, Ernie Stevens and Hilda Davis who founded schools. The Thomas Oliver Robinson Memorial School started by Nellie Robinson, celebrated its 100th anniversary in 1998. The Foundation Mixed School, a primary school, founded by Hilda Davis in 1939, is still in existence.

Education is free and available to all children, and is compulsorily up to the age of sixteen. The nation has a very young population with approximately 44 percent under the age of 25 years. The government, therefore, recognises that it has a mammoth task to educate its youth. The current Minister of Education, the Honourable Bertrand Joseph has declared: "My Government is committed to expanding and enhancing our education system. With increasing globalisation and the CSME (Caribbean Single Market and Economy), the training and retraining of our human resources at all levels is critical. Of particular urgency is the expansion of secondary education. To this end, my Government has resolved to build two new secondary schools within its first five years in office."

Currently, the nation has 64 primary schools catering for children between the ages of 5 and 12. Of this total, 34 are free; owned and operated by the government through its Ministry of Education. Some of the 30 private, fee-paying, primary schools follow international curricula. However, they must also incorporate basic elements of the

J Jones

Jennings Primary School

Caribbean Examinations Council (CXC) awards ceremony for outstanding students

University of the West Indies School of Continuing Studies

national curriculum. There are six primary grades. On attaining Grade Six (at average age 11+) students sit a national Primary School Examination. Successful candidates then progress to the next level of free, secondary education.

Of the sixteen secondary schools in the nation, nine are free, government-owned. Seven are fee-paying, private ones. Secondary school students range in age from 11 to 18 years. They progress through five forms. In Form V, students sit for examinations of Caribbean Examinations Council (CXC) that cover a wide range of subjects. These examinations are roughly equivalent to the British GCE and A-level examinations, the European Baccalaureate, the American High School Diploma and the Canadian Grade 12.

The third tier in the system is the tertiary level. Today, there are four widely recognised institutions offering post-secondary, college and university level education as well as continuing education: The Antigua State College, the University of the West Indies School of Continuing Studies, the Antigua and Barbuda Hospitality Training Institute and the Antigua and Barbuda International Institute of Technology.

The oldest is the Government's Antigua State College that began as a teacher training college for the Leeward Islands. It now has several other departments including a post-secondary Advanced Level Department that prepares students for the Caribbean Examinations Council's CAPE examinations (equivalent to the Cambridge Advanced Level

End of the day at Ottos School

Kirnon School

examinations). Its Undergraduate Department offers University of the West Indies accredited programmes in the Arts and Sciences. Departments of Engineering, Business and Commerce and Schools of Nursing and Pharmacy are also well established there.

The University of the West Indies School of Continuing Studies, the outreach arm of UWI, caters to local needs for distance and continuing education. An important part of its stated mission is its commitment to the process of "continually enhancing the intellectual development of the Caribbean in all spheres".

The Antigua and Barbuda Hospitality Training Institute offers both academic and practical training for the Hospitality Industry. The Antigua and Barbuda International Institute of

Technology is well on its way to becoming a regional institution of excellence in the field of information technology.

As a final note, it must be mentioned that pre-school education is fast becoming a critical sphere of the education system. Approximately 120 of such schools (including day-care centres) currently exist – all privately owned. However, several of the free, government primary schools have kindergarten sections attached to them. At this level, the teaching staff is 100 percent female. Indeed, the teaching profession in Antigua and Barbuda, as it is in many parts of the world today, is predominantly female.

Ermina Osoba, BSc, PhD, is Resident Tutor and Head at University Centre, UWI (University of the West Indies) School of Continuing Studies, Antigua and Barbuda.

Health and well-being

Dr Eumel Samuel

The Healthcare System in Antigua and Barbuda is robust, consisting of Primary Healthcare and Tertiary Healthcare. The Primary Healthcare is extensive and is geared towards affordable medical care for the young and the old. To this end, the Medical Benefits Scheme was established and is in the forefront in the financial aspect of affordable healthcare for all – a tenet of the World Health Organization. At this point in time the Medical Benefits Scheme takes care of certain endemic and chronic diseases and, from all indications, will have a wider coverage in the future.

The endemic and chronic diseases covered by Medical Benefits Scheme includes hypertension, diabetes, cardiovascular diseases and asthma. The beneficiaries of the scheme make a contribution, matched by employers, as a percentage of their wages.

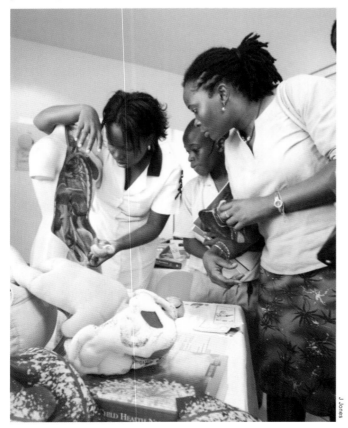

There are some 26 health centres or clinics in Antigua and Barbuda and they function as public healthcare systems. At these clinics, maternal healthcare can be accessed to a level that is the envy of some developing countries. The prenatal and postnatal care of mothers and would-be mothers are extensive. There is monitoring of communicable diseases together with the appropriate treatment of such diseases at a cost borne by the public purse. Laboratory tests are done to screen patients as part of maternal healthcare.

Child Care

Postnatal care is an emblem in the state of Antigua and Barbuda. This programme was instituted more than thirty years ago, and championed by Dr Margaret O'Garra, a paediatrician. The success of this programme is borne out by the fact that more than 95 percent of all infants are vaccinated against childhood and other communicable diseases. This programme has a built-in rigidity in that children are not permitted in public or private schools without the appropriate records of vaccinations. The compliance in this situation is unmatched.

Such a compliance is contributed to the fact that counselling and education form part of the protocol of the primary healthcare system. Counselling and education are not restricted to mothers or would-be mothers, but is extended to fathers and would-be fathers. This is astonishing, compared with other developing countries, but the percentage of fathers attending the clinics for counselling and education is impressive as well as encouraging to healthcare providers.

A commendable development has taken place in the public healthcare system in Antigua and Barbuda. It is the development of three up-scaled health centres. There is an attempt at these centres to offer primary healthcare at higher levels. In this regard, certain acute presentations are no longer referred to the public hospital but are handled efficiently and effectively at these centres. The centres are staffed by full time medical practitioners and a compliment of other healthcare providers. To further augment the primary healthcare system, pharmacy services have been

Mount St John Hospital

Medical Benefits Scheme

Medical Benefits Pharmacy

incorporated into these up-scaled clinics. This allows for the ease with which patients can obtain prescribed medications for their illnesses. In addition, it helps to relieve the pressure from the central pharmacy, operated by Medical Benefits Scheme.

Tertiary Healthcare

Holberton Hospital is the sole public hospital in Antigua and Barbuda. It compliments the primary healthcare systems, offering a wide range of medical services. Surgical procedures are done by highly qualified surgeons, assisted by well-trained and experienced nursing personnel. The laboratory service is extensive and is headed by a qualified pathologist, who is a native to the soil. The other departments of orthopaedics, obstetrics and gynaecology, radiology and paediatrics are well staffed as any other commensurate hospital. Recently, a dialysis programme has been instituted at Holberton Hospital.

Private Healthcare

Private medical institutions are scattered throughout the state offering services comparable to private institutions in any country. Adelin Medical Centre, for example, offers a wide range of medical services. Private laboratory services are also available and include MedPath Laboratory, BellLab Services and Biomedical Lab Services.

Belmont Clinic is a private, standalone diagnostic centre in Antigua offering diagnostic services in radiology and cardiology. It is unique in that it is the only diagnostic centre with MRI services on the island and a full range of echocardiographic services. Other radiological services include CT, ultrasound, mammography, x-rays and fluoroscopy.

The private services complement the public service and, in some cases, may duplicate services offered in the public sector.

In general, the compliment of medical services offered in Antigua and Barbuda, both public and private, surpass many in other developing countries.

Sport and pastimes

Basketball has gained great popularity over recent years

Photogenesis

J Jones

Beach volleyball

J Martin / Photogenesis

Antigua Recreation Ground

Photogenesis

Prime Minister, Baldwin Spencer (left) with cricketing legend, Viv Richards

M Merchant

Prime Minister, Baldwin Spencer congratulates Brian Lara on his record-breaking 400 runs

M Merchant

Brian Lara leaves the pitch at the Antigua Recreation Ground after making his record-breaking 400 runs against England in April 2004. He is followed by West Indies team-mate, Ridley Jacobs

L Joseph

Sporting challenge on the high seas

ANTIGUA YACHT CLUB MARINA & RESORT

Situated in a calm spot in Falmouth Harbour, Antigua Yacht Club Marina and Resort is located within easy walking distance of Pigeon Beach and is a full service marina catering directly to the super-yacht market. As a focal point for yachts in Falmouth, the marina features an integral dingy dock and a range of shops that combine to bring a 'little village' feeling to life in the marina.

Integrated into this Caribbean village-style complex are various boutiques, outdoor cafés, restaurant, art gallery, travel agency, bookstore, liquor store, supermarket, property sales/rental office, marine chandlery, telephone services and a dedicated internet facility. These amenities give the marina a lively, carnival-like atmosphere which encourages visitors to return time and again.

The Antigua Yacht Club is located onsite making this marina the centre of activity for the annual boat show and regattas for which Antigua is world famous. The yacht club also receives a percentage of the dockage fees, a concept which has often been complemented by a number of captains during past seasons.

Situated above the lively Antigua Yacht Club Marina, among beautifully landscaped gardens, is the elegant and sophisticated Yacht Club Marina Resort. The resort is ideal for couples and families looking for an idyllic getaway. This exclusive hillside resort overlooks Falmouth Harbour and features thirty executive suites and an intimate twenty-room boutique hotel. Amenities include a fully equipped fitness centre, spa, Turkish steam bath and a dedicated medical room with first aid and accident and emergency facilities.

T Sprague / Photogenesis

T Sprague / Photogenesis

Photo courtesy Antigua Yacht Club

The ultimate tourism destination

Spectacular view across Coco Bay

A traditional welcome for cruise ship passengers

J Jones

Barbuda

Jumby Bay

Cedar Valley Golf Club

J Jones

Rex Halcyon Cove at Dickenson Bay

Curtain Bluff

Coco Bay

Ffryes Bay

CURTAIN BLUFF

Under the same private ownership for over forty years, Curtain Bluff is a world class Caribbean resort that offers luxurious accommodation, excellent cuisine and quality service. Fabulous junior suites and the lavish Grace Bay and Morris Bay Suites - completed in November 2002 - are considered to be some of the best and most sumptuous in Antigua and, indeed, the Caribbean.

The resort was the first to offer a luxury fully inclusive service which includes all meals, beverages, deep sea fishing, scuba diving and other water sports, tennis, squash, golf putting green, gym and aerobics.

The world famous Antigua Sailing Week, which takes place at the end of each April, was created by the hotel's owner, Howard Hulford, over 35 years ago. Earlier in April, during the Antigua Classic Regatta, over 100 beautiful historical yachts sail by the hotel.

An annual weekly tennis tournament is held in May, boasting a team of professionals including Fred Stolle, Ross Case, Owen Davidson and Kathy Rinaldi, and in November a tennis challenge week is held.

Howard Hulford has also established his own import company to bring in the freshest ingredients and delicacies from around the world. The resort is also home to one of the finest wine cellars in the Caribbean with more than 25,000 bottles.

Locally, Curtain Bluff operates its Old Road Fund which raises money to assist the community with such programmes as teen camps in the United States, the provision of computers and sports equipment, and the awarding of university scholarships.

Photos by Ken Maguire

St James's Club at Mamora Bay

A Granger

A JEWEL IN THE CROWN

Abbott's Jewellery & Perfumery is a one-stop shop for an outstanding selection of jewellery, watches, china, crystal figurines, fragrances and a host of other fine gifts and accessories.

Located in the heart of the Heritage Quay Duty Free Mall in St John's, this Antiguan-owned business carries the most exclusive collections including David Yurman, John Hardy, Roberto Coin and Gucci. It offers a selection of Italian 14k and 18k gold, and a wide, handpicked variety of precious and semi-precious stones.

Internationally renowned Swiss-made watches are on display and the company is an authorised dealer for many leading brands including Rolex, Cartier, Breitling, Omega, Rado, Tag Heuer, Gucci, Raymond Weil and Movado.

As well as the world's finest jewellery and watches, Abbott's stocks extensive selections of fragrances and giftware. These include Kosta Boda, Lladro, Swaroski and Orreford, as well as a fine selection of Cartier accessories.

Jumby Bay

Galley Bay

163

Sandals

CARLISLE BAY

Named 'Hotel of the Year, 2005' by the UK's *Tatler* Travel Guide, Carlisle Bay is a stunning addition to Antigua's diverse hotel sector. With its dramatic backdrop of rolling mountains and rainforest, the hotel's contemporary design is impressive.

All of its eighty suites are spacious and have ocean views. Relaxation and rejuvenation are among the philosophies of Carlisle Bay which offers an exceptional spa (called 'Blue'), yoga and pilates, as well as nine tennis courts and a wide range of water sports.

With two exceptional restaurants – 'Indigo on the Beach' and 'East' (right) – offering the finest cuisine, a futuristic library and a luxurious screening room showing the latest movies, the experience is made complete.

Disney cruise liner at Heritage Quay

Colombian Emeralds, right, at Heritage Quay

CEDAR VALLEY GOLF COURSE

Located at the northern end of Antigua, Cedar Valley Golf Course is just three miles from both St John's and V.C. Bird International Airport, and is within ten minutes' drive of no fewer than ten excellent hotels.

This magnificent, 18-hole course is hilly and offers superb views, particularly from the 2nd, 6th and 13th tees, and from the 12th and 15th greens.

Several holes are of particular interest. The 4th hole is a par 4 downhill from the tee with a dogleg right. There is a pond and a large tree 25 yards left from the tee as well as a grassed bunker in front of the green. The 12th is a par 4 dogleg up a very steep hill. The 14th is a par 4 and is especially attractive with the fairway running in a 'funnel' formed by slopes on either side, and a green framed by trees. The 16th is a par 5 from an elevated tee.

The well maintained golf course has wide fairways and ample cart paths, and is ideal for players of all levels and skills.

Blue Waters

DISCOVER ANTIGUA'S VERY INTIMATE PLACES

Antigua VIP (Very Intimate Places) is a group of small hotels, resorts, inns and guesthouses, each with under fifty-room occupancy. The group comprises thirteen members all offering their own brand of hospitality while ensuring personal attention from their local owner operators and managers.

With superb locations, breathtaking views, fabulous gardens and great beaches, many are off the beaten track; some are located near sites of historical interest, while others are aimed at the business traveller and are located near the capital.

Being locally-owned and managed, and without 'middle-men',

the members take pride in being able to offer a personal and unique service. They are using the internet to reach out to the wider public with the aim of educating visitors to Antigua and Barbuda of their often overlooked accommodations.

Each location offers a special brand of hospitality, combined with an intimate knowledge of the local environment and culture to provide a truly unique and memorable experience. Indeed, many of the owners and managers reside at their properties thus adding to the very intimate and personal service.

Antigua VIP resists the temptation to be mass-marketed or even pre-packaged, fearing that it may compromise its members' personal brand of service, which is as friendly and welcoming as the nation itself.

ANCHORAGE INN

The brainchild of four Antiguan businesswomen, the Anchorage Inn sits on the outskirts of the Dickenson Bay beach area. Following the closure of the original venue - where previously the women had held Christmas parties for Antigua's less fortunate children - the foursome decided to purchase the premises and establish a hotel of their own.

These enterprising women, whose backgrounds include the hospitality industry, insurance and law, wanted to create a place that would be enjoyed by their friends and family. Their personal touch has resulted in a hotel that is brimming with Caribbean flair, ambience and hospitality.

ANTIGUA BEACHCOMBER HOTEL

Situated on the breezy northeast coast of the island, on the fringe of one of Antigua's many beaches, the Antigua Beachcomber Hotel offers an environment of warmth and relaxation.

This locally-owned, 28-room hotel is ideal for holidaymakers and business people alike and is located within five minutes' drive of V.C. Bird International Airport.

A popular venue for wedding ceremonies, honeymoon couples and business conferences, the Antigua Beachcomber Hotel is also renowned for its fine cuisine which is served in its Oceanview Restaurant.

CATAMARAN HOTEL

Established by renowned Antiguan yachtsman, Hugh Bailey, and his family in 1968, the Catamaran Hotel is one of the few truly Caribbean inns left in Antigua. In the tradition of Caribbean families, this small hotel is now being lovingly cared for by his daughter, Feona.

Located at the water's edge at Falmouth Harbour, near the historic Nelson's Dockyard, the inn boasts many repeat guests who are captivated by its beautiful location. The Catamaran Hotel is also a popular choice for couples, honeymooners, families or singles seeking value for money in a welcoming and friendly environment.

The hotel also has a private and secluded beach which is surrounded by lush trees and vegetation providing a relaxing and peaceful hideaway.

TRADE WINDS HOTEL

Situated on a hillside overlooking the spectacular Dickenson Bay, the Trade Winds Hotel is set within lush, landscaped gardens. With its panoramic views, the hotel offers relaxing and peaceful surroundings in an unhurried and friendly atmosphere.

The hotel's Bay House Restaurant is one of Antigua's finest restaurants and offers a tantalizing selection of local, regional and international dishes.

Trade Winds Hotel

Sandpiper Reef Resort

Long Bay Hotel

Anchorage Inn

Antigua Beachcomber Hotel

HARBOUR VIEW APARTMENTS

Overlooking Falmouth Harbour and the Caribbean Sea, Harbour View Apartments is situated within walking distance of a full service marina, fine restaurants and the local supermarket.

Comprising six, split-level accommodations, each apartment includes two bedrooms, bathroom, living room and dining area, and a fully equipped kitchen.

Harbour View Apartments has also provided a base for Antigua Race Week winning crews from the yachts 'Sagamore' and 'My Song'.

OCEAN INN

Nestled within gardens overlooking the historic Nelson's Dockyard, Ocean Inn provides a combined glimpse of luxury, history, geography and tropical elegance.

Surrounded by all the charm and serenity of Antigua's countryside, Ocean Inn is a mere five-minute walk from many restaurants and shops, activities such as sailing, diving, tennis, horseback-riding and deep sea fishing, and the finest beaches and two of the country's most modern marinas.

LONG BAY HOTEL

Long Bay is a small hotel consisting of twenty rooms and five cottages. It has been run by the Lafaurie family since 1966 and is situated on a peninsula with a quiet bay on one side and a beautiful beach on the other.

The cottages are dotted around the landscape and afford privacy, seclusion and are ideally positioned to catch the easterly breeze. The rooms are situated just feet from the bay-side facing east, and guarantee beautiful sunrises and constant Trade Winds.

Most water sports are available at Long Bay including sunfish sailing, windsurfing, kayaking, water-skiing and in-shore fishing. Snorkelling off the beach is a popular activity and there is a protected barrier reef which is ideal for beginners as well as the more advanced diver. The hotel also boasts an all-weather, championship tennis court.

The hospitality at Long Bay Hotel is truly Antiguan with a laid-back and personal touch and its emphasis on comfort and relaxation.

SANDPIPER REEF RESORT

The Sandpiper Reef Resort is one of Antigua's noted beachfront getaways and is a favourite with honeymooners, wedding parties and organisations wishing to book the facilities of an entire resort for their participants.

This intimate and relaxing resort is located no more than ten minutes' drive from V.C Bird International Airport and the many shopping areas within the capital.

Sandpiper Reef comprises 24 beautiful beachfront and ocean-view rooms, including two suites. Each room enjoys a spectacular view and is appointed with king and queen size beds, satellite TV, direct dialling phones and private ocean-view balconies. The resort provides many dining choices including room service. The Reef Restaurant serves an array of fresh seafood, international cuisine and local Caribbean specialities; the Beach Grill offers more casual dining; and the Beach Bar provides snacks and drinks.

WILLOWBY HEIGHTS APARTMENTS

Located in the parish of St Philips, on the south-east coast of Antigua, Willowby Heights Apartments comprises four, single unit apartments overlooking the beautiful Willoughby Bay.

Established in May 2002, Willowby Heights is owned and principally operated by Keithroy Brodie, an Antiguan from the nearby village of Freetown.

CORTSLAND HOTEL

A short walk from downtown St John's, Cortsland Hotel is ideally situated for access to some of Antigua's most historic sites, including Fort St James and St John's Cathedral. The Public Market is nearby, with its local handicrafts and art shops, as well as duty free stores offering some of the best bargains in the Caribbean.

With its prime location and conference facilities for up to two hundred people, the Cortsland Hotel is an ideal choice for business meetings and seminars.

The hotel is also a popular choice for dining out, and is well-known for its West Indian specialities.

Ocean Inn

Trade Winds Hotel

Harbour View Apartments

Willowby Heights Apartments

Catamaran Hotel

Blue Waters

BLUE WATERS

Nestled in fourteen acres of tropical gardens, with its own private bay boasting the option of two beautiful white-sand beaches, Blue Waters is one of Antigua's most secluded tropical escapes.

Originally established around 35 years ago, and now completely refurbished, Blue Waters offers unique personal service and attention to detail from professional management and staff.

The resort offers the choice of luxury rooms, suites or villas, a spa, gym, tennis court and water-sports. In the evening there is the choice of dining in the comfort of the outdoor Palm Restaurant or treating yourself in Vyvien's a la carte restaurant.

Jumby Bay

JUMBY BAY

Jumby Bay (a Rosewood Resort) is a fully inclusive resort set on a 300-acre private island. Surrounded by tropical foliage and pristine white sand beaches, this exclusive location is two miles off the coast of Antigua and is only accessible by boat.

The lush island is noted for its two excellent sunbathing beaches, in addition to winding paths lined with towering palms - ideal for walking or biking.

A haven for naturalists, the island is home to a variety of wildlife including the endangered hawksbill sea turtle.

Jumby Bay is renowned for providing world-class service and distinguished amenities in the most luxurious surroundings.

J Jones

LONG BAY HOTEL

Long Bay is a small hotel consisting of twenty rooms and five cottages. It has been run by the Lafaurie family since 1966 and is situated on a peninsula with a quiet bay on one side and a beautiful beach on the other.

The cottages are dotted around the landscape and afford privacy, seclusion and are ideally positioned to catch the easterly breeze. The rooms are situated just feet from the bay-side facing east, and guarantee beautiful sunrises and constant Trade Winds.

Most water sports are available at Long Bay including sunfish sailing, windsurfing, kayaking, water-skiing and in-shore fishing. Snorkelling off the beach is a popular activity and there is a protected barrier reef which is ideal for beginners as well as the more advanced diver. The hotel also boasts an all-weather, championship tennis court.

Wit its well-stocked library, consisting of around a thousand books, Long Bay also offers many indoor activities including darts, table tennis and board games to keep children as well as adults entertained.

Dinning is a special treat at the Long Bay Hotel. In the main Club House, the Turtle Restaurant provides a full breakfast menu featuring many local fruits. Lunch is served on the terrace at the Beach House Restaurant which offers a diverse menu including local fish dishes. Dinner is generally a global experience featuring North American, European and Caribbean dishes.

The hospitality at Long Bay Hotel is truly Antiguan with a laidback and personal touch and its emphasis on comfort and relaxation.

DIAN BAY RESORT & SPA

Dian Bay Resort & Spa is a secluded retreat on Antigua's eastern coast. From its intimate hillside setting, guests are treated to the spectacular views of the lagoon and the ocean beyond.

The fifty guest rooms are set within lush tropical gardens and they all have their own private balcony. A three-tiered swimming pool adds a unique touch to the surroundings, and the exceptional Caribbean cuisine makes the experience complete.

The full service spa was opened in November 2004, and offers a wide range of treatments and therapies in a serene environment overlooking the azure waters of the lagoon.

CLOTHING LINE IS A LABOUR OF LOVE

British-born Janet Musi arrived in Antigua in 1979 and fell in love with the island and its way of life. Two years later, she launched Jingjok, an import and export company supplying gift shops, hotels and boutiques throughout the region with quality affordable batik.

In 1998, Janet decided to change the line and make it a truly Caribbean product by making all goods in Antigua. The progression was slow; with the batiked fabric arriving in Antigua from Thailand and then to be made into the various items for sale. In 2000, linen sourced from the Caribbean was brought into the Jingjok line and proved to be a popular and successful product. This led to the second phase of the project. With the help of the OECS, a batik specialist from Thailand was enlisted to teach local Antiguans the various techniques of this ancient art form.

Batik is an expressive art form which requires precision and dedication to achieve the colourful and dramatic effects that make each piece unique. To begin with, the linen is stretched onto a frame and a design is then drawn on to it using hot wax, which is applied with a 'tjanting' or brush. Afterwards, each piece is coloured using special dyes and then dried. The fabric is then boiled in soapy water to remove all wax residues before it can be made into the garment or item. The wax acts as a barrier to the various dying processes and can be applied and washed out several times to produce the desired effect.

Jingjok designs and produces various lines of batiked clothing as well as tablecloths, napkins, place settings and cushion covers.

Media for the masses

Joanne C. Hillhouse

Emerging diversity and openness could be said to characterise media in Antigua and Barbuda in the early days of the new millennium, creating exciting times for media professionals and the wider public, who are making the most of this unprecedented access. But the notion of media as the "voice" of the people is a fairly new chapter in a story that began in 1748, when the first publication reportedly came off the presses. Some would argue, and have, that it wasn't until 1943 - with *The Workers Voice* - that the notion of media for the masses began to take hold.

The next chapter would be characterised, in general, by media as a political tool – either via state control or protest. The Antigua Workers Union/Progressive Labour Movement answered the Antigua Trades & Labour Union/Antigua Labour Party's *Voice* with its *Antigua Star* in the late 1960s and 1970s; and the Antigua Caribbean Liberation Movement had its *Outlet*, with noted critic Tim Hector at its helm. There have been others, such as the state-owned *The Nation*, but today only the *Voice* survives – and not prominently. The *Outlet* bowed out in 2004, surviving its 'Fan the Flame' architect by two years.

Today, the front page belongs primarily to the *Daily Observer*, a publication that began as a protest tool by fax in 1993, and the *Antigua Sun*, yin to its yang, dating back to 1997. There is a range of other publications, from *The Sunday Scoop*, which was launched in 2004, to specialist publications dealing with health, youth or pure entertainment. *Essential*, the latest attempt to birth a magazine culture, was launched

BEST OF BOOKS

Located in Redcliffe Street in St John's, Best of Books is Antigua and Barbuda's largest and most comprehensive bookshop. With weekly shipments from the United Kingdom and the United States, the range of books on offer is both diverse and extensive. Categories include cookery, health and well-being, children's books, Caribbean interest, sport, religion, plus a wide selection of fiction.

The company has also launched a new initiative within the store entitled 'Made in Antigua'. As the name suggests, all the items within the range have been locally-produced and include souvenirs, arts and crafts, and limited edition prints by local artists.

in February 2005. At that time tourism minister Harold Lovell complemented the quality of the production and embraced it into the fold as part of Antigua and Barbuda's repositioning as the best brand in Caribbean tourism. *Essential* is a product of Homegrown Publications.

The most dramatic strides in the latter part of the 20th and early 21st centuries, however, have surely been made by the electronic media; and, in particular, radio. Observer Radio is credited with having played a critical role in the 2004 elections by dint of the access it afforded other views.

State-owned ABS radio began broadcasting in the early 1960s and, apart from the religious [Lighthouse] or relay stations [Caribbean Relay], radio remained, for a long time, the almost-exclusive domain of the state. Though private, ZDK, licensed to operate in 1970, and its spin-off, SUN, were owned by and affiliated with the ruling government of the day.

It was Observer Radio that took its battle to the Privy Council and won the right to broadcast in the very first year of the new millennium. Apart from breaking the state monopoly, 91.1 FM altered the landscape in another significant way: Talk Radio, which had languished in the dust of Top 40 radio, became the format of choice across the airwaves – from Crusader [launched by the now ruling United Progressive Party while in opposition] to ABS and ZDK.

Meanwhile, Family Radio and Red Hot, the latter owned by popular jam band Burning Flames, provide a steady fix for those craving music; with GEM – a station broadcasting

from Trinidad, and maintaining a sales office in Antigua – also proving to be quite popular in this genre, with music from the 1980s to present day.

TV is long overdue for a revolution. Broadcast from 1965 throughout the Leeward Islands and owned by Rediffusion International of London, Columbia Broadcasting, and Bermuda Radio and Television, ZAL was acquired by government in 1975 and renamed ABS-TV.

Cable Television Entertainment Systems, which began broadcasting in 1983, was privately owned but government affiliated. And despite having a locally-run channel, it beams mostly foreign (in particular, US-produced) programmes across the island. But in 2004, CTV was acquired by Antigua and Barbuda Investment Bank and Global Bank of Commerce, with plans to develop greater local content via HAMA-TV. The opening up of the cable market, post-2004 elections, also cleared the way for the emergence of Karib Cable.

HAMA Productions, meanwhile, rates a mention given its pioneering efforts in producing local entertainment for the electronic media. HAMA produced Antigua and Barbuda's first and second feature-length films, *The Sweetest Mango* [2001] and *No Seed* [2002] and a number of local edutainment programmes for ABS-TV and the wider Caribbean.

In the seminal year 2004, the media fraternity finally came together under the direction of veteran journalist Colin James to form the Antigua & Barbuda Media Congress. Where these developments will lead, only time can tell.

The political scene

Bruce Goodwin

It can be said that the modern political history of Antigua and Barbuda began in 1951, the year universal adult suffrage was granted the territory by the British colonial overlords. Prior to then, the right to vote in elections was limited to individuals who satisfied certain requirements of property ownership and income. Such requirements excluded the vast majority of Antiguans and Barbudans from participation in the political affairs of their country, since, at that time, the people of this country, for the most part, existed in a state of the most abject poverty and neglect.

While the granting of universal adult suffrage in 1951 reflected a new policy of the British government towards its colonies in the West Indies generally, the vehicle of struggle that the Antiguan and Barbudan people had used to advance their cause was the Antigua Trades and Labour Union (AT&LU), founded in 1939 and led by Vere Cornwall Bird Sr since 1941. Thus, the first really free general elections in the history of Antigua and Barbuda were those of 1951, which resulted in the formation of the first Labour Party government, with Vere Bird Sr as Chief Minister and a Cabinet comprising four of his elected colleagues; Messrs E.H. Lake, E.E. Williams, Machesney George and L. Hurst.

This first labour government is remembered for its integrity, openness and transparency. It inspired great confidence in the people of the country, who were motivated to work hard to redress the disadvantages and absence of opportunity that characterised the post-slavery colonial era that had begun with the abolition of slavery in 1834 and lasted until 1951.

Thus, the first decade of self-government was

Members of the Upper and Lower Houses of Parliament after the opening of the first session following the UPP victory at the polls. Seated (l-r): President of the Senate, Dr Edmond Mansoor, Governor General, Sir James Carlisle, Prime Minister, Baldwin Spencer, Speaker of the House, D. Giselle Isaac-Arrindell and Leader of the Opposition, Robin Yearwood. Second row (l-r): Sen. Francis Nunes, Hon. Charlesworth Samuel, Attorney General, Justin Simon Q.C., Hon. Hilson Baptiste, Sen. Joanne Massiah and Sen. Lenworth Johnson. Third row (l-r): Clerk of Parliament, Sylvia Walker, Sen. Clare Roberts, Hon. Chalah Codrington, Hon. Elston Adams, Hon. Jacqui Quinn-Leandro and Hon. Asot Michael. Fourth row (l-r): Sen. Terry Ephraim, Sen. Colin Derrick, Hon. Dr Errol Cort, Hon. John Maginley, Hon. Harold Lovell, Sen. Chester Hughes, Hon. Bertrand Joseph, Sen. David Massiah, Sen. Anthony Stuart and Sen Gail Christian. Fifth row (l-r): Hon. Gaston Browne, Sen. Davin Joseph, Sen. Elmore Charles, Hon. Winston Williams, Hon. Wilmoth Daniel and Sen. Aziz Hadeed

characterised by a number of highly successful initiatives in the areas of agricultural and industrial development. The Peasant Development Office (PDO), a department of the Ministry of Agriculture, pioneered a new system of land tenure and agricultural development, leading to the empowerment of a new class of independent small farmers that performed in an exemplary manner in the production of food crops, cotton, sugar cane, and small livestock. In these early years, the agricultural production of this sector soared, enabling the people to achieve a good measure of food security and to earn new levels of income that was used to better their social conditions of housing, health care, and education for their children.

Moreover, this first labour government embarked on a progressive programme of industrial development organised by the newly-formed Industrial Development Board (IDB). This organisation founded a number of factories with the goal of creating vertical linkages with the new agricultural sector. Thus, an edible oil factory produced cooking oil and animal feed from the cotton seeds; another factory produced the staple cornmeal from locally-grown corn; while another enterprise produced arrowroot; and a cotton ginnery served the Sea Island cotton industry of the Leeward Islands as the central location to gin the fine cotton and produce seeds for planting. Indeed, Antigua and Barbuda seemed to be firmly established on the road to progress with the formerly disenfranchised people at the helm of their own development.

The next stage of constitutional advancement was to come in 1967 with the status of Statehood in Association with Britain - a sort of halfway house to full independence - where the national government was given responsibility for the state's internal affairs while Britain retained responsibility for defence and external affairs.

However, during the decade of the 1960s, a number of tensions developed in the AT&LU leading in 1968 to that organisation rupturing and a number of its influential leaders forming a new union - the Antigua Workers' Union (AWU). The leader of this new union, former General Secretary of

Prime Minister, Baldwin Spencer speaking at a UPP rally to celebrate the first anniversary of his government in office

Prime Minister, Baldwin Spencer (left) and former Prime Minister, Lester Bird handing over a signed Code of Conduct governing the 2004 general elections to Chairman of the Antigua Christian Council, Bishop Donald J. Reece

the AT&LU, George Walter, would go on to help form a new political party - the Progressive Labour Movement (PLM) - that would challenge the Antigua Labour Party successfully in the general elections of 1971.

Thus, the decade of the 1970s opened with a new government in Antigua and Barbuda. While the early initiatives of the ALP had met with unqualified success, the new social forces unleashed by this very success proved problematic for the then aging leadership of that party. Furthermore, the conflicts that developed as a result of the leadership of the union being, at the same time, the leadership of the national government proved difficult to resolve and contributed significantly to the loss of popularity and confidence that helped motivate the electorate to turn their allegiance to the new PLM party.

Notwithstanding their impressive victory at the polls, however, the new government was bedevilled by an international situation that undermined their efforts to grow the economy and empower the people. For it was at this time in the early 1970s that the global oil market was destabilised, with the advent of the OPEC oil cartel, the rapid increase in oil prices and the resultant shocks to the economies of small states in particular. Thus, the economic and social programmes of the PLM government were undermined by events over which they had no control.

The early 1970s also saw the emergence of a new political force called the Antigua Caribbean Liberation Movement (ACLM), led by prominent activist Leonard Tim Hector. Hector had emerged as a political strategist with the AWU during its struggle with the AT&LU and the ALP during the late 1960s. Later, however, as first Chairman of the PLM, he had clashed with George Walter, the AWU strongman who had decided to seize the opportunity to rise to national leadership as head of a PLM government.

Thus, outmanoeuvred by the erstwhile trade unionist, Hector, a respected intellectual and historian, organised his movement and dedicated his organisation to a certain brand of radical politics and to agitating against the PLM government. The mouthpiece of the ACLM, the weekly *Outlet*

Prime Minister, Baldwin Spencer attended the 25th Meeting of the Conference of Heads of Government of the Caribbean Community which was held in Grenada from 4 to 7 July 2004. The meeting was presided over by Dr the Rt Hon. Keith Mitchell, Prime Minister of Grenada and Chairman of CARICOM.
Seated (l-r): Hon. Roosevelt Skerrit, Prime Minister of the Commonwealth of Dominica, Hon. Said Musa, Prime Minister of Belize, Rt Hon. Owen Arthur, Prime Minister of Barbados, Dr the Right Hon. Keith Mitchell, Prime Minister of Grenada, Dr Edwin Carrington, CARICOM Secretary General, Hon. Baldwin Spencer, Prime Minister of Antigua and Barbuda, Most Hon. P.J. Patterson, Prime Minister of Jamaica and Hon. Dr Denzil Douglas, Prime Minister of St Kitts and Nevis.
Standing (l-r): Dr the Hon. Kenny Anthony, Prime Minister of St Lucia, Hon. Patrick Manning, Prime Minister of the Republic of Trinidad and Tobago, His Excellency Bharrat Jagdeo, President of the Co-operative Republic of Guyana, Dr the Hon. Ralph Gonsalves, Prime Minister of St Vincent and the Grenadines, His Excellency Dr Runaldo R. Venetiaan, President of the Republic of Suriname, Rt Hon. Perry G. Christie, Prime Minister of the Commonwealth of the Bahamas, Hon. Michael Misick, Chief Minister of the Turks and Caicos Islands and Hon. Walter Scott, Premier of Bermuda

newspaper, proved an effective propaganda tool and helped turn public opinion against the PLM regime.

The ALP, meanwhile, reorganised itself in opposition, attracting new blood and new competence into its leadership, in the shape of the leader's two sons, Vere Jr and Lester Bryant, both newly-qualified lawyers, and John St Luce, a graduate economist, along with Hugh Marshall. All four of these "Young Turks" had lived in England during the 1960s and had yearned to return home to participate in political activity. This reorganised and reenergized ALP became the people's choice at the 1976 elections, when it was returned to office with eleven of the seventeen seats in the Lower House of Parliament. One remarkable aspect of this result was the fact that three members of the Bird family – V.C. Bird Sr and his two sons, Vere Jr and Lester Bryant - were now all together members of parliament.

All the parties contesting the 1976 elections had stated their support for Antigua and Barbuda to become an independent nation during the ensuing parliamentary term. As it turned out, it was the ALP that won the opportunity to take the nation into independence in 1981. Independence Day on the 1 November 1981 marked the final break with the British colonial power, and the achievement of full independence for the nation that was officially named Antigua and Barbuda.

The new ALP regime was to govern the country for 28 years continuously until the elections of 2004, when a new political formation - the United Progressive Party (UPP) - would come to power in a landslide victory at the polls.

The first decade of independence was characterised by rapid economic growth that enhanced the popularity of the ALP regime. However, as the years went by, the new regime degenerated into a pattern of mismanagement of the economy that ultimately diminished its base of support and created the conditions that allowed for the emergence of a successful challenge to its leadership of the country.

The PLM that had lost the elections in 1976 continued to decline as a political force. A number of its leaders and supporters had come together in a new political grouping during the 1980s, called the United National Democratic Party (UNDP), led by prominent physician, Dr Ivor Heath. In the elections of 1989, the UNDP candidate for the St John's Rural West constituency, trade unionist Baldwin Spencer, was the only opposition candidate on Antigua to win a seat, with the ALP candidates being victorious in all the other constituencies. Thus, with an impregnable majority in Parliament as the decade of the nineties opened, the ALP had returned to the kind of political hegemony it had enjoyed during the 1950s and early 1960s. Furthermore, the veteran ALP leader, Vere Bird Sr, was now of advanced age and was clearly no longer equal to the task of effectively steering the ship of state. Thus a leadership vacuum had opened at the highest level of state control. A struggle for power in the ALP was therefore imminent.

Government complex

During 1990, a number of civil society organisations and the three opposition political parties (the PLM, UNDP, and the ACLM) began a series of consultations on the state of the political situation in the country. These consultations led to the formation of a coalition of organisations called the National Council of Organisations (NCO). During the year or so that the NCO lasted, its member organisations called for the unification of the opposition parties to confront the ALP hegemony. Out of this call resulted the formation of the United Progressive Party (UPP), a united front of the three opposition parties. Baldwin Spencer, the only member of any of these parties then in parliament was selected leader of the new united party. At its first election challenge in 1994, the UPP gained five parliamentary seats, becoming the official opposition to the ALP, now led by V.C. Bird Sr's son, Lester Bryant.

The 1994 elections were a watershed that indicated clearly that the days of ALP leadership of the nation were numbered. A critical problem confronting the country, however, was the obsolete nature of the electoral system, with an electoral register that had not been revised in over two decades. The issue of electoral reform therefore became the rallying point of opposition forces. The ALP was not to yield on

this issue until it had won yet another election in 1999, after which the calls for electoral reform became so strident that a new electoral system had to be implemented before the country would accept the legitimacy of any other elections.

Thus, the electoral system was reformed and a new electoral register was prepared by an Electoral Commission, a new institution in the management of national elections, during 2003. The stage was therefore set for the general elections of 2004 to be undoubtedly free and fair. These elections led to the first electoral defeat of the ALP in 28 years, and the accession to office of the United Progressive Party, with its leader Baldwin Spencer as Prime Minister.

Lady Joan Shoul and Ambassador Sir David Shoul, from the left, being greeted by Premier Wen Jai Bao during Antigua and Barbuda's state visit to the People's Republic of China. Prime Minister Baldwin Spencer looks on, and in the background are Dr Jacqui Quinn-Leandro, left, and Cisley Solomon

Prime Ministers and Governors-General

Ivor Ford

SIR WILFRED JACOBS

Sir Wilfred Ebenezer Jacobs was born in Grenada on 19 October 1919. His parents were William Henry Jacobs of Cedar Grove, Antigua, and Henrietta Dubois of Grenada. He was the first and only Associated Statehood Governor

of Antigua and Barbuda, the first Governor-General of Antigua and Barbuda, and a former Attorney-General and Puisne Judge of Barbados.

Sir Wilfred was educated at the Anglican Boys' School of Grenada, where his father was Headmaster, and then went on to the Grenada Grammar School for his secondary education.

His decision to pursue a vocation in the legal profession was hindered by the outbreak of the Second World War, which meant that his early legal courses were taken in Grenada. He later travelled to England to do his Bar Finals before being called to the Bar. Sir Wilfred's progress in the legal profession was outstanding. He served in the Federation of the West Indies until its dissolution in 1962. Shortly thereafter, he was appointed as Attorney-General of Barbuda and was later promoted to the Bench as a Resident Puisne Judge.

In 1967, Sir Wilfred was invited to be the first Governor of the Associated State of Antigua and Barbuda. He served in this post for just over fourteen years until - upon the attainment of full independence in 1981 - he was sworn in as the nation's first Governor-General. After twelve years as Governor-General, Sir Wilfred officially retired from active public service in 1993.

Sir Wilfred and Lady Carmen Knight-Jacobs are the parents of three children. He died on 11 July 1995.

SIR JAMES CARLISLE

Antigua and Barbuda's British-styled Constitution calls for the Head of State to be the Queen's personal residential representative, the Governor-General. Currently occupying this important Office of State is His Excellency, Sir James Beethoven Carlisle.

Sir James was born in Bolans, Antigua on 5 August 1937. Obtaining his elementary education in the village school, Sir James entered the teaching profession as a primary school teacher in 1960. One year later, he went to London where he

attended the Workingmen's College and the Northwestern Polytechnic. He also studied at the University of Singapore and the University of Durham in England.

Prior to the royal request to represent Queen Elizabeth II in Antigua and Barbuda, Sir James specialised in Laser Dentistry in Orlando, Florida. The Antigua and Barbudan Head of State is a member of the American Academy of Laser Dentistry; the International Association of Laser Dentistry; and the British Dental Association. From 1961 to 1966, Sir James served in the Royal Air Force. From 1986 to 1990, he was Chairman of the National Parks Authority of Antigua and Barbuda.

In 1993, Sir James Beethoven Carlisle was administered with the Oath of Office of Governor-General of Antigua and Barbuda. In November the same year, he was knighted by the Queen with the Knight Grand Cross of the Most Distinguished Order of St Michael and St George (GCMG). Sir James succeeded Sir Wilfred Ebenezer Jacobs who was the nation's first and longest-serving Governor and Governor-General.

Despite the heavy demands of Office, Sir James makes time to serve as patron of several national organisations which include the Government House Restoration Trust, Clarence House Restoration Trust, the Scout Association, the Red Cross, St John's Ambulance Brigade, the Royal Society, Lion's Club, Rotary Club, the Jaycees and many other social service organisations. Sir James is personally involved with the restoration of the official residence of the Governor-General and also of Clarence House at English Harbour.

Sir James is married to Lady Emma Carlisle and they have five children.

PRIME MINISTER, BALDWIN SPENCER

Winston Baldwin Spencer, the fourth child of Joyce Martin and Frederick Spencer, was born on 8 October 1948 in the suburbs of Antigua's capital, St John's. This quiet, respectful and affable man from Green Bay/Grays Farm (affectionately known locally as 'The Ghetto' or 'The Mud') received his

early education at the Green Bay Government School and later obtained a scholarship to the Princess Margaret Secondary School. This was the first Government school in Antigua and Barbuda to offer free secondary education to the children of low income families.

During his formative years, he was active in the Antigua Trades & Labour Union (AT&LU). He was a member of the Young Juvenile Section of the Union and later, leader of the of the Youth Section of the AT&LU in Green Bay/Grays Farm. Baldwin Spencer's leadership skills were identified by the then President of the AT&LU, the late Sir Vere Cornwall Bird Sr who lobbied the Political Committee of the Union to send young Spencer for training in trade unionism and politics. He excelled at these subjects, thus fortifying his industrial and political future.

The rupture of the AT&LU and subsequent formation of its splinter rival union, the Antigua Workers' Union (AWU) on 31 May 1967, reflected a shrewdness in Baldwin Spencer which has influenced all his thoughts and actions to this day. Upon returning home from training in industrial relations at Ruskin College, Oxford in the UK, the young union field officer dutifully reported to the AT&LU. But subsequent events placed him firmly in the camp of the opposition movement.

Although not prominent in the front line of politics at the time, the young Baldwin Spencer was an important leader of the youth arm of the Progressive Labour Movement (PLM), the political affiliate of the AWU.

In 1989, Baldwin Spencer contested and won the St John's Rural West Parliamentary seat in the general elections. This was against Donald 'DC' Christian, who had occupied the seat since 1976.

In Parliament, Spencer skilfully weathered that first five years of challenges with great dexterity and determination. During this baptism of fire, he found an ally in Hilbourne Frank, the Independent Member for Barbuda. At the birth of the United Progressive Party (UPP) in 1992, Baldwin Spencer was elevated to the Leader's seat. The 1994 general elections pitched the UPP's Baldwin Spencer against the Antigua Labour Party's (ALP) James 'Tanny' Rose. He was again victorious, garnering 1,608 votes against Rose's 842.

And so, after fifteen years' experience in the Antigua and Barbuda Parliament, Winston Baldwin Spencer, on Wednesday, 24 March 2004, was sworn in by Governor-General, Sir James B. Carlisle as the nation's third Prime Minister.

Prime Minister Spencer is married to Jacqui Potter and they have four children.

LESTER BIRD

Lester Bryant Bird was born in the United States on 21 February 1938 and is the third child of the late Sir Vere Cornwall Bird Sr and Lady Lydia Bryant. Like most of his contemporaries, the son of one of Antigua and Barbuda's

most influential leaders attended the Antigua Grammar School where he excelled in sports and athletics.

As a young and physically fit athlete, he represented Antigua and Barbuda and his alma mater nationally, regionally and internationally. In cricket, he was one of the region's most feared fast bowlers. It was the general view at the time that he should have represented the West Indies at Test match level. There were also those knowledgeable sporting experts who felt that he was excellent Olympic material who should have gone further.

His foray into politics followed his athletic achievements, beginning in 1971 when he was appointed leader of the opposition Antigua Labour Party (ALP) in the Senate of Antigua and Barbuda after unsuccessfully contesting the Barbuda seat against Claude E. Francis of the Progressive Labour Movement (PLM). However, in 1976, he was elected to Parliament and was appointed Deputy Premier to his father V.C. Bird Sr. He also served as Minister of Economic Development, Tourism and Foreign Affairs from where he learned the principles of government administration from his experienced father.

On 10 March 1994, Lester Bryant Bird assumed the office of Prime Minister of Antigua and Barbuda after successfully contesting his first general elections as political leader of the ALP. Exactly one decade after his stewardship as Prime Minister, Lester Bird was replaced by the present Prime Minister, Winston Baldwin Spencer of the United Progressive Party (UPP).

In addition to his interest in politics and sports, Lester Bird has revealed another of his latent talents as a poet. In April 2003, he released a book of many of his speeches (*Antigua Vision: Caribbean Reality*) and an anthology of his poetry (*A Bird's Eye View*). The former Prime Minister is also a British-trained lawyer.

SIR GEORGE WALTER

Born on 8 September 1928, into one of Antigua and Barbuda's most famous families, Sir George Herbert Walter is the second of ten children born to Norris and Marietta Walter who lived at the heart of the Capital, St John's.

At seventeen years old, he graduated from the prestigious Antigua Grammar School, and was then invited by his father to manage the family farm at Rendezvous Bay, several miles outside St John's. The following decade of managerial experience was to serve him well during his trade union and political careers.

In 1958, Sir George was chosen to manage and edit the Antigua Trades & Labour Union's (AT&LU) financially-struggling newspaper, *The Workers' Voice*. Within six months, however, the publication was operating at a profit under its young editor and enterprising manager. Two years later, on 4 January 1960, George H. Walter was elected as General Secretary of the AT&LU, replacing Lionel Hurst, who was promoted to the ministerial post of Minister of Labour in a newly-constituted V.C. Bird Government.

After his selection as AT&LU 'Man of the Year' in 1967, he was dismissed as General-Secretary four days later. This executive decision resulted in a serious fracture to the AT&LU that irrevocably altered the industrial and political landscape of Antigua and Barbuda. In 1968, social unrest led to the formation of a new political party - the Progressive Labour Movement (PLM).

Riding on the crest of a popular wave of support, the PLM defeated the Antigua Labour Party (ALP) in the 1971 General Elections, and George H. Walter was sworn in as

the nation's second Premier on Friday, 12 February 1971. Five years later, his party lost the 1976 elections.

His services were acknowledged in the special Millennium Honours List of 2000, with one of the nation's highest awards - the Knight Grand Cross of the Nation (KGCN).

Sir George was married to the late Hyacinth Michael and they had seven children.

VERE CORNWALL BIRD SR

Sir Vere Cornwall Bird Sr was Antigua and Barbuda's first Prime Minister. He was born on 9 December 1909 at New Street, on the southern fringes of the capital, St John's. He was the fourth of five children of Barbara Edghill and Theophilus 'Thophy' Bird. The young Vere Bird was educated at the St John's Boys' School.

He joined the Salvation Army and was sent to Jamaica for training. This opportunity offered him the chance to visit several islands in the Caribbean, where he was able to witness the deplorable living conditions in which the people were compelled to live.

In 1939, V.C. Bird was one of a number of Antiguans and Barbudans who were privileged to attend a meeting convened at the Anglican Cathedral School Room on Long Street. This meeting was at the instigation of Sir Walter Citrine, a member of the Royal Commission that was sent to the region to investigate the root causes of riots that engulfed the entire region in the late 1930s. The Commission was headed by Lord Moyne, a respected member of the House of Lords in the British Parliament.

On 16 January 1939, the momentous decision was taken to form a trade union in Antigua and Barbuda and, shortly thereafter, the Antigua Trades & Labour Union (AT&LU) was born. However, it was not until 3 March 1940 that the union was officially recognised under the Trades Union Act. The first President of the new union was Reginald St Clair Stevens, a businessman in St John's. In 1942, V.C. Bird became the second President of the AT&LU. Soon after his ascension to the presidency of the AT&LU, a decision was taken by the union that V.C. Bird should seek election to the Legislative Council. This was successfully achieved in 1946.

In January 1960, Vere Cornwall Bird Sr was appointed the first Chief Minister of Antigua and Barbuda. This new responsibility was a result of constitutional improvement for the territory. As Chief Minister, V.C. Bird was in command of the political structure in Antigua and Barbuda.

From the powerful position of leadership and influence of the work force and the machinery of Government, he became even more powerful, both on the labour front and at the legislative level.

In 1962, following the dissolution of the Federation of the West Indies, V.C. Bird extended a formal invitation to the leaders of the Windward and Leeward Islands and Barbados to join him in Antigua in search of a solution to the problems created by the withdrawal of both Trinidad and Tobago and Jamaica from the Federation. The feeling at the time was that the remaining eight nations should form another federation without the involvement of the larger territories. This group was to be known as 'The Little Eight'.

On 27 February 1967, another constitutional improvement was instituted when Antigua and Barbuda assumed a new status of Independence in Association with Great Britain. This unique model of parliamentary democracy was known as 'Associated Statehood'. It meant that the government of Antigua and Barbuda was responsible for all internal national matters while London retained responsibility for external affairs and defence.

However, the new Premier's greatest political challenge was the serious fracture of the AT&LU which caused a parting of the ways between V.C. Bird Sr and one of his chief lieutenants, George H. Walter, the then dismissed General-Secretary of the AT&LU. The split brought into existence an opposition force of such magnitude that it precipitated a hasty retreat from political office of the hitherto seemingly invincible political arm of the AT&LU, the Antigua Labour Party (ALP).

The turbulent period between 1967 and 1976 was a traumatic time for the ALP and its companion organisation, the AT&LU. In 1971, the ALP lost the General Elections and was only able to retain four of the seventeen seats in Parliament. The leadership of V.C. Bird Sr was tested because of the overwhelming support of the newly-established Progressive Labour Movement (PLM) which was led by George H. Walter. However, V.C. Bird triumphed in 1976 when he was handed the baton of power, once again, by the electorate.

Five years later, and one year into his successive election victory at the polls, Antigua and Barbuda gained independence from Britain and Vere Cornwall Bird Sr received the Instruments of Independence from Britain's Princess Margaret on Sunday, 1 November 1981.

And so, after holding the position of Prime Minister of Antigua and Barbuda for twelve years, Vere Cornwall Bird Sr voluntarily gave up the seat of political power. Six years later, the 'Father of the Nation' died on Monday, 28 June 1999. He was the recipient of the country's highest national award, 'National Hero'. He was also one of the first CARICOM citizens to be awarded the Order of Caricom.

Vere Cornwall Bird Sr, the nation's first Prime Minister, died at the age of 89, having served his native Antigua and Barbuda for more than 54 years.

GOVERNMENT HOUSE, OFFICIAL RESIDENCE OF THE GOVERNOR-GENERAL

The building now known as Government House was originally owned by Thomas Nosbury Kerby, a well known merchant. It is believed that it was built in 1750 and was used as a parsonage until 1800 when it was acquired by the British Government as a residence for the Governor of the Leeward Islands. The following year, the first Governor to take up residence was Lord Lavington.

The building was extended and built upon in order to provide adequate accommodation for the Governor. Further additions since 1801 have transformed the old parsonage into the imposing building it is today. However, the mainly wooden structure has suffered the ravages of time and a restoration programme has been embarked upon in order to preserve one of the country's greatest historic assets.

To date, 35 Governors have lived in the building including noted individuals such as Governor Fiennes, who built the State-run Senior Citizens Home, and Governor T. Reginald St Johnston, who attempted to improve the quality of housing in Antigua by building the model village of St Johnston's.

But perhaps the most well-known and best-loved of all the colonial Governors was Governor Oliver Baldwin (1948-50), 2nd Earl Baldwin of Bewdley. He implemented many social changes in order to improve the lives of Antiguans and Barbudans and was largely responsible for improving the nation's fresh water supply. He was the first Governor to invite a Black person to an official function at Government House, and also encouraged the development of steelband music.

He returned to England on completion of his tour of duty and died in 1958. However, before his death he requested that his body be cremated and his ashes buried in Antigua. His tomb is situated on New Castle Hill.

The economy

Petra Williams

Antigua and Barbuda is a twin-island nation located in the Eastern Caribbean. Best known as a tourism destination and famous for its 365 beaches, it is also an international yachting centre and home to Antigua Sailing Week, one of the world's leading three regattas.

The country has a democratic government modelled upon Britain's Westminster System. The Head of State is the Queen of England who is represented locally by Governor General, Sir James Beethoven Carlisle. Since the country's independence in 1981, the Prime Minister is the Head of Government. The Prime Minister and other members of the lower house are chosen during elections which are constitutionally due every five years. The most recent elections were held in 2004 and saw the election of a new government – the United Progressive Party (UPP) – under the leadership of a new Prime Minister, Hon. Winston Baldwin Spencer. This election victory replaced the Antigua and Barbuda Labour Party (ALP) which had dominated the country's political landscape for the past 28 years.

Over the last five years, Antigua and Barbuda experienced cyclical fluctuations in the rate of economic growth, with real GDP (market prices) growth as low as 1.49 percent in 2001 and recovering to 4 percent by 2003. The nation's economy is heavily services oriented, with tourism being the main engine of growth. Construction, financial and government services are also major contributors to the economy.

Photo: J Martin / Photogenesis

Deepwater Harbour

Gift shop in Redcliffe Quay

J Jones

The offices of Antigua and Barbuda Social Security

J Martin / Photogenesis

Jolly Harbour

J Martin / Photogenesis

Tourism and tourist-related activities account for more than 60 percent of the economy's foreign exchange earnings. In 2003, visitor expenditure was an estimated US$300 million accounting for 40 percent of the country's GDP. When combined with tourism-related expenditure in the transportation and other sectors, total foreign exchange estimates climb to US$525 million or just under 70 percent of all goods and services produced in the economy (GDP).

Construction is the second largest contributor to the Antiguan economy, accounting for 14 percent of real gross domestic output in 2003. A major component of this sector is Foreign Direct Investment (FDI). Direct investment in Antigua and Barbuda has been experiencing steady growth over the past five to eight years. Total foreign direct investment into Antigua and Barbuda is estimated at US$93.3 million in 2003 and preliminary estimates for 2004 suggest that FDI was in excess of US$100 million.

The Government has actively pursued Foreign Direct Investment as a vital component of the country's growth strategy and has instituted a review of all existing processes and legislations relating to attracting and retaining regional and international investment. To this end, the Government is in the process of establishing a one-stop-shop for investors - the Antigua and Barbuda Investment Authority (AIA) - which will function as an investment promotion and facilitation agency. This agency will provide all investors with all pertinent information to facilitate investing in Antigua and Barbuda. Working in tandem with the AIA will be the soon to be incorporated Antigua and Barbuda International Marketing Corporation to jointly promote the twin-island nation regionally and internationally. The collaborative effort will result in a more responsive and investor-friendly climate.

There are also specific concessions aimed at encouraging the development of the hotel industry. The government will be revising the incentives currently offered under the existing Hotel Ordinances Act designed to provide generous and competitive concessions to encourage foreign direct investment in the tourism industry.

Antigua and Barbuda has emerged as an attractive offshore financial centre. The major offshore services offered are banking, trust, international business corporations, gaming and a ships registry. The offshore jurisdiction is governed by the International Business Corporations (IBC) Act (Amended) 2004, the Consolidated Money Laundering Prevention Act (MLPA) of 1996, and the Merchant Shipping Act. The twin-island nation has also signed up to the Financial Action Task Force and the Caribbean Financial Task Force Recommendations. The Financial Services Regulatory Commission (FSRC) and the Office of National Drug Control Policy (ONDCP) are the executing agencies of the government's international financial regulatory mechanism.

The existing regulatory and compliance environment is equal to or stronger than most international financial centres due to continuous amendments and revisions to make the jurisdiction internationally compliant.

In addition to the regulatory environment, the relatively tax-free nature of the Antigua-Barbuda jurisdiction ensures that it remains competitive. All international business corporations are fully exempt from direct taxes in respect of any international trading, investment or commercial activity including corporate and personal income tax, withholding tax and stamp duties.

There is also a strong supporting infrastructure to encourage foreign investment. There are presently seven

Exhibition and Cultural Centre

commercial banks in operation in Antigua and Barbuda as well as experienced attorneys, accountants and financial consultants. A wide range of technical and financial skills are available within the local workforce. Furthermore, the government has a fairly liberal labour policy, where companies are able to recruit unavailable skilled workers from other jurisdictions.

Business communications are well developed in Antigua and Barbuda. The country's sole international airport is serviced by major airlines with regular scheduled flights to and from Europe, North America and the Caribbean. These airlines include Air Canada, American Airlines, British Airways, Continental, British Midland International, Virgin Atlantic and BWIA. Antigua and Barbuda is also a regional hub for Caribbean Star and LIAT. There is also significant corporate and private aircraft traffic which is catered for by Fixed Based Operations (FBO) companies that operate private facilities in close proximity to the airport. There is also regular transportation by air and sea between Antigua and Barbuda. Antigua and Barbuda recently signed a Memorandum of Understanding with the Peoples Republic of China awarding Special Status to visitors from that country to travel as tourists to Antigua and Barbuda.

Antigua also has a well developed maritime transportation sector. The country is currently serviced by eleven shipping lines from most major ports of call. The main cargo landing facility is the Deep Water Harbour, where cargo landed totalled an estimated 717,041 tons in 2004. The country also plays host to some of the world's largest cruise ships, and it is internationally renowned for its yachting centres.

In telecommunications, the island's telephone services consist almost entirely of fibre optic cable providing a state-of-the-art network. And express courier services are readily available to and from Antigua.

The government is a significant contributor to the country's economic growth. It is the largest employer, with a workforce that consists of just under one-third of the country's labour force. The government is also the single largest investor in the country's infrastructure development. Up until July 2004, it owned the second largest block of hotel rooms. The thrust of the new administration has been to streamline government involvement to being the facilitator rather than the engine of economic growth. In keeping with this thrust, the government is in the process of divesting many of the state's major assets. The sale of the 300-plus room Royal Antiguan Hotel, is evidence of the government's commitment.

As part of the government's role as a facilitator, it is addressing the need for incentives for small business development and ways to stimulate the manufacturing sector. The government has also made significant strides in addressing the large public sector debt.

Aerial photograph of V.C. Bird International Airport taken with the assistance of Caribbean Helicopters   Photo: Photogenesis

ST JOHN'S DEVELOPMENT CORPORATION

St John's Development Corporation is a statutory body enacted by Parliament in 1986 with the aim of developing the nation's capital city in order to improve the quality of life for residents and visitors alike.

In 1987, the Corporation fulfilled its mandate with the construction of the Heritage Quay Duty Free Shopping and Entertainment Complex. Heritage Quay was the first phase of the revitalization of St John's. This project breathed new life into the city and created an area for world class duty free shopping. Today, Heritage Quay offers an extensive range of products to suit every taste. More than fifty shops carry an array of items that include exotic Caribbean arts and craft, souvenirs, perfumes, jewellery, watches, clothing, liquors, cigars, leather goods and electronic items. The Complex also comprises a pier which accommodates all types of cruise ships including the mega cruise liners. The area is a hub for tourist activity and is a significant contributor to the Antigua and Barbuda cruise tourism product.

Also located at Heritage Quay is the Heritage Hotel, a superior business and tourist class hotel which also offers the finest conference facilities. The hotel is conveniently close to the downtown business centre, banks, restaurants, supermarkets, travel agencies and the Duty Free Complex.

Adjacent to Heritage Quay is the Vendors Mall, which is the most recent of the corporation's projects. Here, vendors display a wide variety of their wares, including souvenirs, local arts and crafts, and t-shirts, in an environment which epitomises the traditional hustle and bustle of a Caribbean marketplace.

Lower Market Street has been transformed with the construction of the new Public Market complex, another facility managed by the St John's Development Corporation. The Public Market offers a variety of fresh fruit, vegetables and other dry food items, clothing and crafts. The craft market offers many types of leather goods, shell work, souvenirs, hand-made crafts, t-shirts and locally-made soaps, to name a few. This popular venue is acknowledged to be among the finest of its kind in the Caribbean.

Across the bay is the Multipurpose Cultural Centre which features an Exhibition Centre, Cultural Centre and a Conference Room. This facility is a popular venue for hosting regional and international events such as trade shows, conferences, exhibitions, cultural events and other functions including wedding receptions and graduation ceremonies.

Art and Crafts Market

THIRTY YEARS OF NON-STOP SERVICE

For more than thirty years, the West Indies Oil Company Ltd has been supplying oils, gas, lubricants and LPG to the people of Antigua and Barbuda. The company prides itself on giving excellent service and reliability in the delivery of high grades of fuel and any type of petroleum product.

The West Indies Oil Company operates several strategically-located, 24-hour service stations throughout the nation as well as specializing in the supply of LPG for homes and hotels. It also offers competitively-priced bunker fuels for boats, a waste oil collection service, and is a member of the US Clean Caribbean Co-operative.

The company has also established a local property development company - Friars Hill Development – into which it has invested more than EC$30m. This subsidiary company has provided new homes and employment for Antiguans as well as housing and rental accommodation for visitors and inward investors.

CARIBBEAN ALLIANCE INSURANCE

With its head office in St John's, Caribbean Alliance Insurance is a West Indian regional insurance company that also has agencies throughout the Caribbean.

A sound and well-structured insurance company, it has the experience to meet the hazards and diverse needs of the Caribbean and its people.

HERITAGE HOTEL

Located on the waterfront in downtown St John's, the Heritage Hotel is ideally situated for both tourists and business people. At the heart of the nation's main commercial centre, the hotel is nestled amid a variety of duty free shops and delightful restaurants. With spectacular views over the St John's harbour, the spacious and well appointed executive rooms and suites are air-conditioned and have cable television and telephone. A free internet service is also available.

As a conference centre, the Heritage Hotel offers spacious and private facilities equipped with VCR, television, flip charts and overhead projectors. The hotel's Guest Services agents are available to arrange day tours by boat or air, island excursions, car rentals, horse-back riding, golfing or any other entertainment requirements.

Heritage Hotel was established in 1987 with twenty executive suites and a small meeting room. In 1999, the construction of a new wing added another 26 rooms and a more spacious, fully equipped conference centre. From its inception, the Heritage Hotel has maintained a very high standard in accommodation and service and it now boasts the highest percentage of repeat visitor business in Antigua. Further expansion of its facilities is planned for the near future.

V.C. Bird International Airport

SCOTIABANK

With over 200 branches throughout the Caribbean, Scotiabank is a leading bank in the region, offering a full range of retail banking services and selected commercial finance services. Scotiabank maintains a presence in Antigua and Barbuda through its two branches in St John's and Perry Bay.

BUILDING SOLID PARTNERSHIPS

"No one ever attains very eminent success by simply doing what is required of him; it is the amount and excellence of what is over and above the required that determines the greatness of ultimate distinction."
Charles Kendall Adams

The ABI Financial Group is a network of affiliated companies providing services in banking, investment, insurance, trust and brokerage, real estate development and resort management. With its global and innovative vision, the Group offers current and prospective clients new opportunities in all these areas towards building long-lasting and solid partnerships.

Managed by a team of professional executives with extensive experience in all its areas of service, the Group boasts a high level of commitment, ethical principles and sound management. These qualities have contributed significantly to its rapid growth and increasing success.

Located in the heart of downtown St John's, the companies of the Group are based in its brand new headquarters on Redcliffe Street. With more than one billion dollars of assets under management, ABI Financial Group is the leading financial conglomerate in Antigua and Barbuda.

CABLE & WIRELESS

Cable & Wireless is one of the world's leading international communications companies and the leading provider of communications in the Caribbean.

With operations in twelve Caribbean nations, the company provides mobile, voice, data and IP (Internet Protocol) services to business and residential customers, as well as services to other telecoms carriers, mobile operators and providers of content, applications and Internet services.

The company's principal operations are in the United Kingdom, continental Europe, Asia, the Caribbean, Panama and the Middle East.

Deepwater Harbour

KEEPING THE NATION ON THE MOVE

Harney Motors Ltd (HML) is the longest established and the first indigenous car dealership in Antigua and Barbuda. From small beginnings in March 1970, when the company primarily serviced and repaired vehicles, Harney Motors has grown into a full service automotive dealer.

Shortly after opening, the company was awarded the prestigious Toyota franchise with the first shipment of vehicles arriving in December of that year. By acquiring this dealership, HML became the nation's first distributor of Japanese cars. Along with this new sales operation, a spare parts department was also opened. In 1989, the company underwent major renovations and also introduced its hire-purchase department for the financing of its used (trade-in) vehicles.

In 1985, the Mitsubishi dealership was acquired and a subsidiary company - Ace Enterprises Ltd - was established. The company continued to grow and expand and in 1996, following the acquisition of the Ford dealership, another subsidiary - Galaxy Motors Ltd - was formed. In the same year, Harney Motors received the Kia and Asia dealerships, and in 1999 the company was appointed as the authorised dealer for Mazda.

Today, Harney Motors Ltd is one of the leading car dealerships in Antigua, with modern and attractive facilities and showrooms for new and used cars. The company provides first class after sales service with its technical staff being trained overseas annually by the respective manufacturers. HML also invests substantially in the latest technology and tools to complement the training and expertise of its technical staff. The operation is further enhanced by a comprehensively-stocked spares department.

WORKING WITH GOVERNMENT TO BOOST TOURISM AND COMMERCE

The Stanford Group of Companies is a vibrant part of the economic and cultural life of Antigua and Barbuda. Business activities within the group range from Bank of Antigua, Stanford International Bank and Stanford Trust Company to Stanford Development Company, Sun Printing and Publishing and Caribbean Star and Sun Airlines. Behind them all is a vision to help advance the development of Antigua and Barbuda into a leading, world-class brand name in Caribbean tourism and a premier centre of finance, commerce and services.

Stanford has engaged in high-quality tourism and commercial development that has advanced this vision while reflecting Antiguan and Barbudan culture and enhancing the nation's beauty and environmental riches. An example of this commitment is the Stanford Development Company's one-of-a-kind design and construction projects at V.C. Bird International Airport. Located on sixty acres, these improvements have greatly enhanced the gateway to the country, adding new infrastructure while providing facilities for tourism and commerce for international and regional visitors and investors. Always sensitive to the environment, this project increased the level of vegetation in the area and included the installation of a unique bio-filtration system to reduce waste.

Beginning in 2005, Stanford commenced an innovative programme with the government called the Alliance for Education and Empowerment. Highlights include significant investments in the National Library and a $25 million state-of-the-art secondary school complex, as well as promotion of private entrepreneurship through a special $10 million fund.

Main picture: Overview of proposed airport master plan and, above, the Stanford marsh bio-filter

GLOBAL FINANCIAL CENTRE

With a distinctive Caribbean image, Global Financial Centre is the corporate head office of the oldest licensed bank in the nation's international financial sector, Global Bank of Commerce, as well as the island's newest domestic financial institution, Caribbean Union Bank. Both banks provide wealth management, e-commerce and electronic payment systems to their respective markets.

Located on the Friars Hill Road, the Financial Centre also houses EC Tech Inc., a technology service provider and data centre, which supports the growth and development of modern financial services locally and regionally.

J Jones

LIAT

Considered to be a true Caribbean institution, LIAT has been serving the region for almost fifty years.

The Caribbean airline currently has a network of nineteen destinations that stretches from the Dominican Republic in the north to Guyana in the south.

With its flexible flight schedule, LIAT connects the islands and brings together the diverse flavour, colour, splendour and culture of the Caribbean.

KHOULY ALLIANCE

Since arriving in Antigua and Barbuda in the late 1960s, the Khouly family has grown from strength to strength.

John Khouly was the first to arrive and after years of hard work, established a furniture manufacturing business. He invited his younger brother, George, to join him and he soon took charge of the business and helped it to develop further.

The hard work ethic has always been a driving force within the Khouly family, but the importance of a good education has been paramount. This is no better reflected in the achievements of all their offspring.

John's five children – Joseph, Raymond, Salem, Jack and Jenny – have backgrounds in pharmacology, civil engineering, insurance, accountancy and finance and banking. And George's four children - Jerry and Jimmy, Jessy and Sandy – have backgrounds in civil engineering and architecture, medicine and lawyer.

Through hard work, foresight and commitment to their adopted home, the Khouly family has been a major contributor to the development of Antigua and Barbuda.

J Martin / Photogenesis

West Bus Station

FRANCIS TRADING

Francis Trading Limited was established in April 1972 by Sir Eustace and Lady Rita Francis. From its modest beginnings, the company has grown into one of the nation's leading customs brokers, cargo and cruise ship agents and stevedore contractors.

THE MAP SHOP

Situated on Lower St Mary's Street, The Map Shop is a veritable treasure trove selling maps, charts, prints, and cruising and travel guides of the Caribbean. It has an Educational Department which covers many subject areas including the history of Antigua and Barbuda and other islands in the region.

The Map Shop also sells a wide range of books including many by Caribbean authors and publishers.

SHOUL'S TOYS, GIFTS & HOUSEWARE

Located in the heart of St John's, Shoul's Toys, Gifts & Housewares is one of the largest and longest established businesses in Antigua.

As one of the most popular shopping centres in the capital, the company is also a household name throughout Antigua and Barbuda.

安提瓜和巴布达:天堂一隅

安提瓜和巴布达，人口不多，彼此关系友好亲切，大家总爱说：'若要寻根问祖，个个都是自家人呢。'时至今日，亲朋好友每有团圆喜庆欢聚一堂时，但见融合着多个族裔，有多米尼加共和国棕色面孔，亦有传统黑人、白人以及阿拉伯族裔等，仿如小联合国。

回说当年，我们的一些祖父先辈为了寻找经济发展机会，远赴圣多明哥开采蔗园，很多人从此音讯杳然，直至一些后人重返故土，并带来众多源自西班牙语的名字，于是学校内英语名字的学生与西班牙语名字的学生成为好朋友的现象比比皆是，大家融洽地生活。

在周末市场，安提瓜妇女们要么光顾多米尼加人开设的小摊档，要么逛过黎巴嫩人或叙利亚人的店铺，然后光顾西班牙人的发廊为参与星期日早上的教堂聚会而美容一番，再到华人开设的鸡肉杂碎外卖店或牙买加人的烤肉食肆购买饭菜。

很久以前，这个占地 170 平方英哩（440 平方公里）的双岛之国，已经沉沉实实地建立了一个多国多种族人士聚居的融洽社会，而且彼此水乳交融。

新近移居此地的人士，除西班牙人、华人、非洲人、圭亚那人、牙买加人外，也有为数不多几百

无论如何，旅游业仍是安提瓜和巴布达最大的行业，各地酒店林立，接待各个阶层的游客。由顶级酒店 Curtain Bluff，享誉全球的 Sandals，以至本地经营的 Jolly Beach Resort（本地最大型物业），还有以亲切待客著称的名为 VIP 的小酒店，正是样样俱全。这里阳光灿烂、充满热带风情的小岛，拥有着闻名世界的美丽海滩 -- 安提瓜的洁白沙滩胜地和巴布达纯净、淡红的沙滩美景，一共不下 365 处。而后者亦以富有环保特色的礁湖驰名，无数军舰鸟候鸟群在那里栖息，而大量黄占鹿也都遍野皆是。

到安提瓜和巴布达旅游，直航交通非常方便，进出此间国际机场的各大航空公司不胜枚举，有美航、加航、英航及维珍航机，而加勒比海各航班如 BWIA、LIAT 及 Caribbean Star 亦定期来往各地。对于商务旅客来说，先进的通信设备，包括宽带网络及直拨国际长途电话等，以及会议设

名美国白人和欧洲白人，而他们说起来在人数比在这里土生土长的葡萄牙及苏格兰商人的后代还多。正如当年哥伦布发现新大陆之旅一样，有些人士路过此地就毅然留下来，在东南面 English Harbour/Falmouth/Cobbs Cross 一带，以及愈来愈多地在西南部 Jolly Harbour 等地风光美丽如画的渔业社会过着新生活。

人口正在不断蓬勃发展，逐渐散居全岛各地，昔日的甘蔗园及牧牛场已告湮没。竖立在荒废蔗园硕果仅存的一些古老风车，正见证着农业衰落，代之而起的是各式各类不那么劳动密集型的行业，诸如银行、保险、通信及航空业，随而也出现了一个稳固的中产阶级。

在东加勒比群岛各国中，安提瓜和巴布达于 1983 年率先与中华人民共和国建立外交关系。自从那时起两国关系良好，在国际舞台上相互支持。多年来，中国总共提供了 3.3 亿元人民币的援助，资助了许多建设项目如多功能文化与展览中心、YASCO 运动中心、Greekside 大桥，以及在 Darkwood 的高速公路改进工程。在新的相互合作协议中，中国将资助安提瓜和巴布达，建造一个新的板球运动场，该运动场工程将在 2007 年板球世界杯举行前竣工。预期两国关系将在平等互利的基础上得到继续发展，并为两国人民带来更多的福祉。

施，都能使阁下寓旅游于工作中，真是一举两得。

邮轮游客更大可趁途经此地在首都的免税码头轻松购物，既可在那里众多一流餐馆享受美食佳肴，亦可遨游 Fort Shirley 的历史古堡遗迹以及精心保存的乔治亚时代博物馆船厂 Nelson's Dockyard；又可骑马驰骋，在大西洋跟黄绍鱼一起戏水游泳，或在东北海岸划独木舟，各得其所。

随着本地居民生活日渐富裕，休闲活动也愈来愈见多采多姿。然而，人们对某些娱乐消遣始终一直乐此不疲，而且历久不衰。旅居国外的安提瓜人和巴布达人士喜爱于每年七八月间回国，藉以欢度嘉年华节。这被称为"加勒比海最大的夏季节期"，前后十一天，安提瓜到处一片欢腾，众人都别出心裁精心粉墨装扮，活力充沛的钢鼓乐随处可闻，而加力骚韵律的音乐则时而悠扬悦耳，时而讥刺热烈，往往令人捧腹大笑；街头巷

2004 年 11 月安提瓜和巴布达总理 W. Baldwin Spencer 对中国进行官方访问时与中国驻安巴大使任小平在长城合影。

由中国援助修建的中国-安提瓜和巴布达友谊大桥

由中国援助修建的中国-安提瓜和巴布达友谊大桥

中国驻安巴大使任小平会晤安巴驻中国大使 David Shoul。

尾都见大跳宣泄狂热的舞蹈，不分种族信仰和阶级，人人都玩过痛快。

而巴布达亦有同类性质的在年初举行的嘉年华节，称为'加勒比嘉年华'（Caribana）。安提瓜人纷纷奔往这姊妹岛欢度周末，饱餐一顿精选大螯虾、鲜蟹、海螺或鹿肉美食。

在四月间，此间的航班大概最为繁忙的了。木球大赛和帆船比赛周往往都在这时举行。在屡创佳绩的安提瓜康乐场 (Antigua Recreation Grounds)，不但木球赛事本身大受捧场，而且不论赢输，整日的杯觥交错，美食佳肴和悠扬乐韵等各类聚会活动，已足以令人乐而忘返。安提瓜人素有热情好客的美誉，在此更加表露无遗，难怪球迷们年年都乐于旧地重游。

帆船比赛周 -- 世界主要帆船大赛之一 -- 吸引全球各地赛帆运动好手及赛迷纷纷前来，English Harbour、Falmouth Harbour 和 Jolly Harbour 各个港口地区到处洋溢着一片欢乐气氛。同时，在 Falmouth Harbour 亦举行展出全球最豪华游艇的春季船展，对于富豪买家以至看得着迷的参观人士说来，都会是一次难得的体验。

最新的节庆"回家节"是在 2004 年独立日首次举行的。庆祝活动主题环绕社群尊严、国家传统和标志、以及各个深具意义的历史事件。此外，回家节亦举办各项娱乐活动，包括分区选美、福音演唱会及大型餐舞会。鉴于节庆活动圆满成功，预料今后将会年年都举行。

安提瓜人和巴布达人传统上信奉基督教，所以无论星期六晚玩到多晚，星期日还是会踊跃前往教堂做礼拜。圣公会圣约翰教堂是市内最大教堂，亦有循道公会、莫拉维亚会、天主教会、复临安息日会、浸信会、卫理公会、路德会、五旬节会等各个教堂，而一些较小规模的宗教团体，例如巴哈派教徒、穆斯林和印度教徒，都在此间和睦共处。

各个教会除了满足人们精神需要之外，在保存文化方面亦扮演着重要角色。例如，圣公会和莫拉维亚会所举办的食品节，便已成为全国性的活动，烹调厨艺跟各类展品和美食享用互相辉映。每逢这类活动，移民社群都能大显身手，日本料理寿司、多米尼加山鸡美食、蒙特塞拉特岛的焖炖嫩肉 (Montserratian kiddie stew)、以及来自基特达岛的一种强肾植物洋菝契食品，都纷纷出炉，叫人大快朵颐。同时，地道美食，例如泡腌米(血肠)布丁、海豚鲱鱼、用面粉、甜马铃薯及椰油制成的面团，以及煮鳕鱼等都非常受欢迎呢。

这些活动不单在于替教会进行筹募善款，亦实实在在表现着人们的自我肯定和重建信念；即是：尽管在来自北美的价值观念、有线电视及国际网络不断耳濡目染之下，我们在躯体上、在心底上，以及在灵性上，仍然是不折不扣的西印度群岛人。

安提瓜和巴布达 - 事实和数据

名称 : 安提瓜和巴布达

首都 : 圣约翰

面积和位置 : 安提瓜是英语通行的各个'背风群岛'(Leeward Islands) 中面积最大的海岛，长约 14 英哩(23 公里)，阔 11 英哩(18 公里)，面积约为 108 平方英哩(280 平方公里)。最高点为 Boggy Peak，海拔1319 英呎(402 米)。巴布达位于安提瓜以北约 30 英哩(48 公里)，为一地形平坦的珊瑚岛，面积约为 68 平方英哩(176 平方公里)。

安提瓜和巴布达位于东加勒比海'背风群岛'(Leeward Islands) 中央，在赤道以北约北纬 17 度。南面为蒙特塞拉特岛和瓜德罗普岛，北面和西面为尼维斯岛、圣基特斯岛、圣巴特斯岛和圣马丁岛。

气候 :气温由冬季月份华氏 70 多度(摄氏 21 度)，至夏天为 80 多度。年均降雨量只有 45 吋(114 厘米)，常年处于低湿度，是东加勒比海群岛中阳光最灿烂的地方。

国家元首: 英国女王伊利莎白二世，总督詹姆斯.卡莱尔总督为代表。

总理: 鲍德温.斯潘塞

人口: 77,000 (2003 年联合国数字)

语言: 英语

货币:东加勒比海元(EC$)； 美元 (US$) 亦接受

国际拨号 : +1268

国际网络网域 : ag

电力 :岛上部分地区 110 伏特，其余地区 220 伏特。多数酒店两种电压通用。

银行 : Antigua and Barbuda Development Bank, Antigua and Barbuda Investment Bank, Antigua Commercial Bank, Bank of Antigua, Bank of Nova Scotia, First Caribbean International Bank, Global Bank of Commerce, RBTT Bank, Royal Bank of Canada.

医疗设施: 设有一间医院及一间私家诊疗所，并有多名全科医生及专科医生执业。岛上各地均有配药服务。

安提瓜和巴布达总督 James B. Carlisle (中间者)、副总理 Wilmoth Daniel、中国驻安提瓜和巴布达大使任小平在 Jolly Beach 渡假胜地庆祝中华人民共和国成立 55 周年。

护照和入境: 美国、加拿大和欧盟国民须出示公民身份证明(有效护照或经认证出生证)。其它国家居民可联系他们就近的旅游办事处查询入境规定。

航空旅游

V.C. Bird International Airport 是旅客乘搭航班抵达安提瓜和巴布达的入境点。从北美洲经圣胡安及圣马丁均有直航及接驳航班开达，而欧洲亦每日有几个班次到达。设有定期及包机服务前往多个邻近海岛。

飞行时间:纽约 - 4 小时； 迈阿密 - 3 小时； 多伦多 - 4 小时；波多黎各 - 1 小时； 伦敦 - 8 小时； 法兰克福 - 9 小时； 巴黎 - 8 小时。

服务北美线航班 : Air Canada、American Airlines、BWIA、Continental Airlines、US Air.

服务英国线航班 : BWIA、British Airways、Virgin Atlantic 和 Sunsail Airways，均有接驳前往欧洲其它各地。

岛际航班 : LIAT, Air St Kitts/Nevis、Carib Aviation、Caribbean Star Airlines、Montserrat Airways、Caribbean Sun.

海上旅游

邮轮停泊码头位于圣约翰港及首都心脏地带的Heritage Quay。

旅游办事处

美国

安提瓜和巴布达旅游及贸易部
Antigua and Barbuda Department of Tourism and Trade
25 S.E. 2nd Avenue, Suite 300, Miami, FL 33131

电话：305-381-6762
传真：305-381-7908
电邮：cganuear@bellsouth.net

安提瓜和巴布达旅游部
Antigua and Barbuda Department of Tourism
610 Fifth Avenue, Suite 311, New York, NY 10020

免费专线：888-268-4227
电话：212-541-4117
传真：212-541-4789
电邮：info@antigua-barbuda.org

安提瓜和巴布达大使馆
Embassy of Antigua and Barbuda
3216 New Mexico Avenue NW, Washington, DC 20016

电话：202 362 5122
传真：202 362 5225
电邮：embantbar@aol.com

加拿大

安提瓜和巴布达旅游及贸易部
Antigua and Barbuda Department of Tourism & Trade
60 St Claire Avenue East, Suite 304, Toronto, Ontario, M4T 1N5

电话：416-961-3085
传真：416-961-7218
电邮：info@antigua-barbuda-ca.com

英国

安提瓜和巴布达旅游办事处
Antigua and Barbuda Tourist Office
15 Thayer Street, London, W1U 3JT

电话：(44) 20 7486 7073
传真：(44) 20 7486 1466
网页：www.antigua-barbuda.com
电邮：antbar@msn.com

德国、奥地利、瑞士和北欧

安提瓜和巴布达旅游部
Fremdenverkehrsamt Antigua und Barbuda
Thomasstr. 11, D-61348 Bad Homburg, Germany

电话：49-6172-21504
传真：49-6172-21513

法国

安提瓜和巴布达旅游办事处
Office du Tourisme D'Antigua et Barbuda
43 Avenue de Friedland, Paris 75008

电话：33 (0) 1 53 75 15 71
传真 33 (0) 1 53 75 15 69

意大利

安提瓜和巴布达旅游部
Dipartimento del Turismo di Antigua e Barbuda
Via Santa Maria alla Porta, 9, 20123 Milan

电话/传真：(039) 02 877 983
电话（有关旅游业务）：(039) 02 720 987 27

安提瓜和巴布达

安提瓜和巴布达旅游部
Antigua and Barbuda Department of Tourism
Government Complex, Queen Elizabeth Highway, St John's

电话：268-462-0480
传真：268-462-2483
电邮：deptourism@antigua.gov.ag

安提瓜酒店及游客协会
Antigua Hotels & Tourists Association
Island House, New Gates Street, P.O. Box 454, St John's

电话：268-462-0374
传真：268-462-3702
电邮：ahta@candw.ag

Antigua-et-Barbuda : un petit bout de paradis

On disait autrefois de la petite société d'Antigua-et-Barbuda, dont les membres sont proches les uns des autres, que « Si l'on remonte assez loin dans le passé, tout le monde est parent avec tout le monde. » Aujourd'hui, ceux qui étaient partis sont revenus pour de grandes retrouvailles avec leur famille, et l'on voit ainsi certains habitants à la peau brune de la République dominicaine rejoindre la population traditionnelle noire, blanche ou arabe.

Il y a bien longtemps, nos grands-pères et leurs frères, en quête d'opportunités économiques, partirent à Saint-Domingue pour couper la canne à sucre. Dans la plupart des cas, on n'entendit plus jamais parler d'eux, jusqu'à ce que leurs descendants reviennent pour réclamer leur patrimoine. C'est pourquoi, dans les classes des écoles primaires, des Davis sont aujourd'hui assis à côté de Diaz, et des Pena sont amis avec des Peters.

Le samedi, les Antiguaises achètent au marché des légumes aux marchands dominicains, se rendent à pied dans les quartiers chics pour faire des courses dans des magasins libanais ou syriens, puis vont en grand nombre dans des salons de coiffure espagnols pour être bien coiffées le dimanche matin, avant d'aller chercher un plat chinois de chop suey au poulet ou de porc « jerk » à la jamaïcaine.

En avance de nombreuses années sur le mouvement d'intégration, cette nation formée de deux îles, d'une superficie de 440 km², est une société multiraciale et multi-ethnique issue de différentes nations.

Parmi les nouveaux immigrants (Espagnols, Chinois, Africains, Guyanais et Jamaïcains), on trouve des centaines d'Américains et d'Européens blancs, maintenant plus nombreux que les descendants, nés ici, de marchands portugais ou écossais. Certains, comme Christophe Colomb, sont venus en voyage de découverte, mais ont décidé de jeter l'ancre – souvent dans les petits ports pittoresques d'English Harbour, Falmouth ou Cobbs Cross dans le sud-est et, de plus en plus, de Jolly Harbour dans le sud-ouest.

La population, en pleine croissance, occupe maintenant toute l'île, et l'on trouve à présent des villages là où étaient jadis plantés des champs de canne à sucre et des pâturages pour les vaches. Les moulins abandonnés – seuls vestiges des anciennes plantations sucrières – témoignent du déclin de l'agriculture au profit d'autres industries nécessitant moins de main-d'œuvre comme la banque, l'assurance, les télécommunications et l'aéronautique, qui ont contribué à l'émergence d'une classe moyenne forte.

C'est toutefois le tourisme qui reste la principale industrie d'Antigua-et-Barbuda. Les nombreux hôtels – du prestigieux Curtain Bluff à l'hôtel Sandals de renommée mondiale, en passant par le Jolly Beach Resort (un établissement géré au niveau local qui est aussi la plus grande propriété du pays), ou encore les auberges VIP (very intimate places, ou lieux très intimes) – s'adressent à toutes les catégories de clientèle. Bénéficiant de la fraîcheur des alizés, ces îles inondées de soleil offrent certaines des plus belles plages du monde : 365 véritables joyaux au sable blanc à Antigua et des plages de rêve immaculées au sable rose à Barbuda. L'île sœur possède également un lagon très bien préservé qui abrite une réserve protégée où l'on trouve des frégates et une population de daims.

Grâce à l'aéroport international qui accueille de grandes compagnies aériennes comme American Airlines, Air Canada, British Airways et Virgin Atlantic, mais aussi des compagnies antillaises telles que BWIA, LIAT et Caribbean Star, il est possible de se rendre facilement et directement à Antigua-et-Barbuda. Et pour le voyageur d'affaires, les équipements de télécommunications de pointe (tels que l'Internet haut débit et le téléphone international direct) et les installations pour conférences font quasiment des voyages d'affaires d'agréables vacances.

Quant aux passagers des paquebots de croisière, ils profitent de leur escale pour faire des achats dans les boutiques hors taxes du port de la capitale, pour dîner dans les nombreux et excellents restaurants, pour visiter des sites historiques comme les ruines du fort Shirley et Nelson's Dockyard (chantier naval de Nelson et son musée dans un bâtiment du XVIIIᵉ siècle restauré) ; ils font aussi du cheval, nagent avec les raies pastenagues dans l'Atlantique ou longent la côte nord-est en kayak.

Le niveau de vie des habitants ayant augmenté, les activités de loisirs ont pris de l'ampleur et se sont diversifiées. Mais certaines distractions sont presque sacrées. Les Antiguais et les Barbudais de l'étranger viennent séjourner dans leur patrie en juillet et août, au moment du carnaval, que l'on qualifie de « plus grand festival d'été des Caraïbes ». Onze jours durant, Antigua s'amuse en célébrant cette fête avec des mascarades hautes en couleur, de la musique de steel band pleine d'énergie, des airs de calypso aux paroles douces et/ou satiriques et des danses de rue libératrices qui balaient d'un coup les différences de race, de religion ou de classe.

Pour le carnaval de Barbuda, appelé Caribana, qui a lieu plus tôt dans l'année et dont l'organisation est semblable à celui d'Antigua, les Antiguais vont à l'île sœur pour y passer un week-end agrémenté des saveurs du homard, du crabe, du lambi ou de la venaison.

Le moment où les arrivées par avion sont les plus

nombreuses est sans doute le mois d'avril, époque où ont généralement lieu les matches internationaux de cricket et la Semaine de la voile. Le cricket, pratiqué sur un terrain qui a fait date dans l'histoire (l'Antigua Recreation Grounds), constitue un véritable festival en soi, où le fait de gagner ou de perdre n'est qu'un détail de ces journées de fête que l'on passe à boire, manger, rire et écouter de la musique. C'est ici que l'hospitalité et l'amabilité bien connues des Antiguais sont les plus visibles, comme vous le diront les passionnés qui reviennent chaque année.

Quant à la Semaine de la voile – où se dispute l'une des plus grandes régates du monde –, elle attire des amoureux de la voile des quatre coins de la planète, transformant ainsi English Harbour, Falmouth Harbour et Jolly Harbour en centres où règne une activité fébrile. Le Salon nautique de printemps, où sont présentés à Falmouth Harbour les bateaux les plus luxueux du monde, est un grand moment autant pour ceux qui achètent que pour ceux qui regardent émerveillés.

« Homecoming », le tout dernier festival, a été organisé pour la première fois en 2004 pour la fête de l'indépendance. Les festivités ont tourné autour de la fierté communautaire, des institutions et symboles nationaux, ainsi que d'événements historiques importants. Elles ont également été l'occasion de divertissements tels que des concours de beauté locaux, une fête du gospel et un banquet de gala où l'on pouvait danser. Vu le succès qu'a connu ce festival, il aura vraisemblablement lieu chaque année.

Les Antiguais et les Barbudais sont de tradition chrétienne, et quelle que soit l'heure à laquelle la fête du samedi soir s'est terminée, le nombre des fidèles présents à la messe du dimanche est en général élevé. Outre la cathédrale anglicane de Saint John's qui domine la ville, des églises de confession méthodiste, morave, catholique, adventiste, baptiste, wesleyenne, luthérienne et pentecôtiste coexistent pacifiquement avec des assemblées de fidèles moins nombreux comme les bahaïs, les musulmans et les hindous.

En plus d'être les gardiennes des âmes, les églises contribuent à préserver la culture. Les foires alimentaires anglicane et morave, par exemple, sont des manifestations nationales où la nourriture est tout autant exposée que consommée. C'est là que les communautés d'immigrants se réalisent pleinement, en offrant de délicieux plats aussi variés que les sushis japonais, le *mountain chicken* dominicain, le ragoût *kiddie* de Montserrat et la salsepareille (aphrodisiaque) de Saint-Kitts. Et des plats locaux très prisés comme le boudin au riz mariné, l'alose à la farine de maïs et le poisson salé au *doucana* (boulettes aux fruit secs) ne se conservent bien sûr que très peu de temps.

Ces manifestations ne permettent pas seulement aux églises de collecter de l'argent, elles nous donnent la possibilité de nous affirmer et nous rassurent sur le fait que, malgré la montée des valeurs nord-américaines, la télévision par câble et l'Internet, nous restons antillais là où cela compte, c'est-à-dire dans notre ventre, dans notre cœur et dans notre attitude.

Antigua-et-Barbuda - Faits et chiffres

Nom : Antigua-et-Barbuda

Capitale : Saint John's

Superficie et situation géographique : Antigua, la plus grande des îles Sous-le-Vent anglophones, mesure 23 km de long sur 18 km de large, pour une superficie d'environ 280 km². Le point le plus haut est Boggy Peak, qui s'élève à 402 m. Barbuda, située à quelque 48 km au nord d'Antigua, est une île corallienne plate d'une superficie d'à peu près 176 km².

Antigua-et-Barbuda se situe au milieu des îles Sous-le-Vent, dans l'est des Caraïbes, à 17 degrés environ au nord de l'équateur. Au sud, se trouvent les îles de Montserrat et de la Guadeloupe et, à l'ouest et au nord, Nevis, Saint-Kitts, Saint-Barthélemy et Saint-Martin.

Climat : les températures vont approximativement de 23° C en hiver à 29° C en été. Il pleut en moyenne 1 140 mm seulement par an, ce qui en fait les îles les plus ensoleillées des Caraïbes orientales, avec une faible humidité toute l'année.

Chef de l'Etat : la reine Elisabeth II, représentée par le gouverneur général sir James Carlisle

Premier ministre : Baldwin Spencer

Population : 77 000 habitants (ONU, 2003)

Langue : anglais

Monnaie : dollar des Caraïbes de l'est (EC$) ; le dollar des Etats-Unis (US$) est également accepté

Indicatif international : +1268

Domaine Internet : .ag

Electricité : dans une partie de l'île, le courant est de 110 volts et dans le reste, il est de 220 volts. La plupart des hôtels sont équipés pour les deux voltages.

Banques : Antigua and Barbuda Development Bank, Antigua and Barbuda Investment Bank, Antigua Commercial Bank, Bank of Antigua, Bank of Nova Scotia, First Caribbean International Bank, Global Bank of Commerce, RBTT Bank, Royal Bank of Canada.

Equipements médicaux : il y a un hôpital et une clinique privée, ainsi que de nombreux médecins généralistes et spécialistes. Des services de pharmacie sont disponibles partout sur les îles.

Passeport et immigration : les ressortissants des Etats-Unis, du Canada et de l'Union européenne doivent être en mesure de prouver leur nationalité (passeport en cours de validité ou extrait d'acte de naissance certifié conforme). Les résidents des autres pays doivent s'informer des formalités d'entrée auprès de l'office de tourisme le plus proche.

VOYAGES EN AVION

L'aéroport international V.C. Bird est le point d'entrée des voyageurs arrivant en avion à Antigua-et-Barbuda. Il existe des vols directs et des correspondances au départ de l'Amérique du Nord via San Juan et Saint-Martin, ainsi que plusieurs vols quotidiens depuis l'Europe. Des vols réguliers et charters desservent de nombreuses îles voisines.

Durée de vol : New York - 4 h ; Miami - 3 h ; Toronto - 4 h ; Puerto Rico - 1 h ; Londres - 8 h ; Francfort - 9 h ; Paris - 8 h.

Compagnies aériennes desservant l'Amérique du Nord : Air Canada, American Airlines, BWIA, Continental Airlines, US Air.

Compagnies aériennes desservant le Royaume-Uni : BWIA, British Airways, Virgin Atlantic et Sunsail Airways, avec des correspondances vers l'Europe.

Compagnies assurant des vols inter-îles : LIAT, Air St Kitts/Nevis, Carib Aviation, Caribbean Star Airlines, Montserrat Airways, Caribbean Sun.

VOYAGES EN BATEAU

Le port de Saint John's et Heritage Quay, au cœur de la capitale, peuvent accueillir les paquebots de croisière.

Offices DE TOURISME

Etats-Unis

Antigua and Barbuda Department of Tourism and Trade
25 S.E. 2nd Avenue, Suite 300, Miami, FL 33131

Tél. : 305-381-6762. Fax : 305-381-7908
Email : cganuear@bellsouth.net

Antigua and Barbuda Department of Tourism
610 Fifth Avenue, Suite 311, New York, NY 10020

Appel gratuit : 888-268-4227. Tél. : 212-541-4117
Fax : 212-541-4789. Email : info@antigua-barbuda.org

Embassy of Antigua and Barbuda
3216 New Mexico Avenue NW, Washington, DC 20016
Tél. : 202 362 5122. Fax : 202 362 5225
Email : embantbar@aol.com

Canada

Antigua and Barbuda Department of Tourism & Trade
60 St Claire Avenue East, Suite 304, Toronto, Ontario, M4T 1N5

Tél. : 416-961-3085. Fax : 416-961-7218
Email : info@antigua-barbuda-ca.com

Royaume-Uni

Antigua and Barbuda Tourist Office
15 Thayer Street, London, W1U 3JT

Tél. : (44) 20 7486 7073. Fax : (44) 20 7486 1466
Site Internet : www.antigua-barbuda.com
Email : antbar@msn.com

Allemagne, Autriche, Suisse et Nord de l'Europe

Fremdenverkehrsamt Antigua und Barbuda
Thomasstr. 11, D-61348 Bad Homburg, Allemagne

Tél. : 49-6172-21504
Fax : 49-6172-21513

France

Office du Tourisme d'Antigua-et-Barbuda
43, avenue de Friedland, 75008 Paris

Tél. : 33 (0) 1 53 75 15 71
Fax : 33 (0) 1 53 75 15 69

Italie

Dipartimento del Turismo di Antigua e Barbuda
Via Santa Maria alla Porta, 9, 20123 Milan

Tél./fax : (039) 02 877 983
Tél. (pour les professionnels du voyage) : (039) 02 720 987 27

Antigua-et-Barbuda

Antigua and Barbuda Department of Tourism
Government Complex, Queen Elizabeth Highway, St John's

Tél. : 268-462-0480. Fax : 268-462-2483
Email : deptourism@antigua.gov.ag

Antigua Hotels & Tourists Association
Island House, New Gates Street, P.O. Box 454, St John's

Tél. : 268-462-0374. Fax : 268-462-3702
Email : ahta@candw.ag

Antigua und Barbuda: Ein Stückchen Paradies

Von der kleinen, eng verwobenen Gesellschaft Antiguas und Barbudas wurde früher gesagt: „Wenn man weit genug zurückgeht, sind *alle* miteinander verwandt". Inzwischen sind viele der ursprünglichen Verwandten aus anderen Gegenden zurückgekehrt, so dass sich braune Gesichter aus der Dominikanischen Republik unter die traditionell schwarze, weiße und arabische Bevölkerung mischen.

Auf der Suche nach Arbeit gingen vor langer, langer Zeit unsere Großväter und ihre Brüder nach Santo Domingo, um dort Zuckerrohr zu schneiden. Von vielen wurde nie wieder gehört, bis ihre Nachkommen heimkehrten, um ihr Geburtsrecht geltend zu machen. Die Namen verraten ihren Ursprung: In den Klassenzimmern der Grundschule sitzen heute Davis und Diaz nebeneinander und sind Pena und Peters beste Freunde.

Auf dem Samstagsmarkt feilschen Antiguanerinnen mit dominikanischen Verkäufern um Gemüse, gehen dann zum Einkaufen in libanesischen und syrischen Läden ins obere Stadtteil, lassen sich anschließend in spanischen Friseursalons ihre Sonntagsfrisur legen, bevor sie auf dem Heimweg ein Hähnchen Chop Suey oder ein jamaikanisches Jerk-Schweinefleisch-Gericht mitnehmen.

Allen Integrationsbewegungen um Lichtjahre voraus, ist dieser 440 Quadratkilometer große Doppelinselstaat, ohne viel Aufhebens darum zu machen, eine multinationale, multrassische Vielvölkergemeinschaft.

Unter den neueren Einwanderern – den Spaniern, Chinesen, Afrikanern, Guyanesen und Jamaikanern – befinden sich auch Hunderte von weißen Amerikanern und Europäern, die jetzt den hier gebürtigen Abkommen portugiesischer und schottischer Kaufleute zahlenmäßig überlegen sind. Manche kamen wie Kolumbus auf Entdeckungsreise, beschlossen aber auf Dauer vor Anker zu gehen – oft in den malerischen Fischerdörfern English Harbour/Falmouth/Cobbs Cross im Südosten und immer mehr auch in Jolly Harbour im Südwesten.

Die wachsende Bevölkerung hat sich über die Insel ausgebreitet und Gegenden besiedelt, die früher Zuckerrohrplantagen und Rinderweiden vorbehalten waren. Verlassene Windmühlen – die einzigen Überreste des ehemaligen Zuckeranbaus – sind Zeugen des Rückgangs der Landwirtschaft und des Aufkommens anderer, weniger arbeitsintensiver Industriezweige wie Bankwesen, Versicherungen, Telekommunikation und Luftfahrt, die dazu beigetragen haben, eine solide Mittelklasse entstehen zu lassen.

Der Tourismus ist und bleibt jedoch die Haupteinnahmequelle von Antigua und Barbuda, und es stehen zahlreiche Hotels für alle Besucherklassen zur Verfügung – vom exklusiven Curtain Bluff und dem weltberühmten Sandals über das lokal betriebene Jolly Beach Resort (der größten Hotelanlage des Landes) bis hin zu VIP-Gasthäusern (Very Intimate Places). Die von kühlenden tropischen Brisen umwehten, sonnengetränkten Inseln besitzen einige der spektakulärsten Strände der Welt: 365 weißsandige Kleinode auf Antigua und einsame Buchten mit rosarotem Sand auf Barbuda. Die Schwesterinsel kann sich auch einer unverdorbenen Lagune rühmen, die ein gut gehegtes Schutzgebiet für Fregattvögel und Damwild bildet.

Über seinen internationalen Flughafen, der von großen Fluggesellschaften wie American Airlines, Air Canada, British Airways und Virgin Atlantic sowie von karibischen Airlines wie BWIA, LIAT und Caribbean Star angeflogen wird, ist Antigua und Barbuda einfach und direkt erreichbar. Und für Geschäftsreisende sorgen fortschrittliche Telekommunikationen (inkl. Broadband-Internet und internationale Telefon-Direktdurchwahl) und Konferenzeinrichtungen dafür, dass ihnen die Arbeit mehr wie Urlaub vorkommt.

Kreuzfahrtpassagiere nutzen unterdessen ihre Landausflüge zum Shopping in den Duty-Free-Läden der Hauptstadt, speisen in den vielen ausgezeichneten Restaurants, erkunden historische Stätten (z.B. die Ruinen von Fort Shirley, Nelson's Dockyard, ein restauriertes georgianisches Museum und einen Boatyard), gehen reiten, schwimmen mit Stachelrochen im Atlantik oder fahren an der Nordostküste Kajak.

Im Zuge des steigenden Wohlstands der Inselbewohner hat sich das Freizeitangebot vergrößert und diversifiziert. Gewisse Aktivitäten sind allerdings immer noch geradezu heilig. Im Ausland lebende Antiguaner und Barbudaner planen ihre Heimatbesuche vorwiegend für die Monate Juli und August, um beim Karneval – dem „großartigsten Sommerfest der Karibik" – mit dabei zu sein. Dann wird in Antigua elf Tage lang gefeiert – mit bunten Maskeraden, rhythmischen Steelbands, romantischen und/oder satirischen Calypsoliedern und kathartischen Straßentänzen, die alle Rassen-, Glaubens- und Klassenunterschiede beiseite fegen.

Für den ähnlich strukturierten Karneval von Barbudas, Caribana genannt, der früher im Jahr abgehalten wird, machen sich die Antiguaner zu ihrer Schwesterinsel auf, wo sie ein Wochenende köstlicher Schlemmerei mit Hummer, Krabben, Muscheln und Wildbret erwartet.

Die meisten Fluggäste kommen jedoch im April, der Zeit des Test Cricket und der Segelwoche. Cricket im historischen

Antigua Recreation Grounds ist schon ein Festival für sich, bei dem die Entscheidung über Sieg oder Niederlage fast nebensächlich ist – angesichts der ganztägigen Partys, bei denen gegessen, getrunken, gelacht und viel Musik gemacht wird. Hier wird die berühmte antiguanische Gastfreundlichkeit besonders augenfällig, wie die Jahr um Jahr wiederkehrenden Fans bescheinigen werden.

Die Segelwoche ihrerseits – eine der führenden Regatten der Welt – lockt Yachties und Bootsliebhaber aus aller Welt an und macht English Harbour, Falmouth und Jolly Harbour zum Mittelpunkt fieberhafter Aktivitäten. Die Frühlings-Bootsschau, auf der in Falmouth Harbour die luxuriösesten Boote der Welt zu sehen sind, ist ein einzigartiges Erlebnis sowohl für Käufer als auch staunende Zuschauer.

Zum Unabhängigkeitstag wurde 2004 erstmalig ein neues Festival mit dem Namen „Homecoming" veranstaltet. Gefeiert wurden dabei der Stolz auf die eigene Gesellschaft, auf nationale Institutionen und Ikonen sowie wichtige historische Ereignisse. Zur Unterhaltung trugen Schönheitswettbewerbe, ein „Gospelfest" und ein Gala-Bankett mit Tanz bei. Aufgrund seines Erfolgs ist anzunehmen, dass das Festival zu einem jährlichen Event werden wird.

Die Antiguaner und Barbudaner sind traditionsgemäß Christen, und ganz egal bis wie spät in die Nacht hinein am Samstagabend gefeiert wurde, sind die Kirchen am Sonntagmorgen doch meist gut gefüllt. Zwar beherrscht die anglikanische Kathedrale von St. John's das Stadtbild, doch auch Methodisten, Moravianer, Katholiken, Adventisten, Baptisten, Wesleyaner, Lutheraner und Mitglieder der Pfingstgemeinden koexistieren friedlich miteinander und mit den kleineren Gemeinden der Baha'i, Moslemen und Hindus.

Die Kirche hütet jedoch nicht nur Seelen sondern trägt auch zur Bewahrung der Volkskultur bei. Die anglikanische und die moravische Lebensmittelmesse sind beispielsweise nationale Veranstaltungen, auf denen zu gleichen Teilen ausgestellt und verzehrt wird. Hier machen sich vor allem auch die Einwanderer nachdrücklich bemerkbar und bieten vielerlei Köstlichkeiten an – von japanischem Sushi über dominikanisches Berghuhn und montserratischen Ziegeneintopf bis hin zu Sarsaparilla, einem Aphrodisiakum der Kittitians. Natürlich wird auch bei lokalen Speisen wie Souse (gepökelte Schweinepfoten) mit Reis, Black Pudding (Blutwurst), Funghi (Maisbrei) und Shadfisch oder Doucana (Brei aus Kokosnüssen & Süßkartoffeln) mit Salzfisch kräftig zugelangt.

Diese Veranstaltungen dienen nicht lediglich der Spendenbeschaffung – sie sind vielmehr eine sehr reale Bestätigung für uns, dass wir trotz des Umsichgreifens nordamerikanischer Werte, trotz Kabelfernsehen und Internet immer noch da Westindier sind, wo es wirklich zählt – im Magen, Herzen und Geist.

Antigua & Barbuda - Fakten & Zahlen

Name: Antigua und Barbuda

Hauptstadt: St John's

Größe & Lage: Antigua, die größte der englischsprachigen Inseln über dem Wind, ist bei einer Fläche von zirka 280 km² etwa 23 km lang und 18 km breit. Der höchste Punkt der Insel ist Boggy Peak, der sich 402 m über dem Meeresspiegel erhebt. Barbuda, etwa 48 km nördlich von Antigua, ist eine flache Koralleninsel mit einer Fläche von zirka 176 km².

Antigua und Barbuda befinden sich in der Mitte der Inseln über dem Wind in der östlichen Karibik, etwa 17 Grad nördlich des Äquators. Südlich von ihnen liegen die Inseln Montserrat und Guadeloupe, nördlich und westlich liegen Nevis, St Kitts, St Barts und St Martin.

Klima: Die Temperaturen rangieren von zirka 23 Grad Celsius in den Wintermonaten bis zu zirka 30 Grad im Sommer. Der jährliche Niederschlag beträgt lediglich 114 cm, was die Inseln zu einer der sonnigsten Gegenden der östlichen Karibik mit ganzjährig niedriger Luftfeuchtigkeit macht.

Staatsoberhaupt: Königin Elizabeth II, vertreten durch den Generalgouverneur Sir James Carlisle

Premierminister: Baldwin Spencer

Bevölkerung: 77.000 (Quelle: UN 2003)

Landessprache: Englisch

Währung: Ostkaribischer Dollar (EC$); US-Dollar (US$) werden ebenfalls akzeptiert.

Internationale Telefonvorwahl: +1268

Internet-Domäne: .ag

Netzspannung: 110 V in einigen Teilen der Inseln, ansonsten 220 V. Die meisten Hotels haben beide Netzspannungen.

Banken: Antigua and Barbuda Development Bank, Antigua and Barbuda Investment Bank, Antigua Commercial Bank, Bank of Antigua, Bank of Nova Scotia, First Caribbean International Bank, Global Bank of Commerce, RBTT Bank, Royal Bank of Canada.

Medizinische Versorgung: Es gibt ein Krankenhaus und eine Privatklinik sowie zahlreiche Allgemein- und Fachärzte. Apothekendienste stehen überall auf den Inseln zur Verfügung.

Reisepässe & Einreise: Staatsangehörige der USA, Kanadas und der EU benötigen einen Staatsbürgerschaftsnachweis (gültiger Reisepass oder Geburtsurkunde). Staatsangehörige anderer Länder sollten sich im Reisebüro nach den für sie geltenden Einreisebestimmungen erkundigen.

ANREISE AUF DEM LUFTWEG

Besucher, die mit dem Flugzeug in Antigua und Barbuda eintreffen, landen auf dem Flughafen V.C. Bird International. Er wird von Nordamerika aus sowohl direkt als auch über San Juan und St Martin angeflogen, und es gibt mehrere Flüge täglich aus/nach Europa. Zu vielen der Nachbarinseln bestehen Linien- und Charterflugverbindungen.

Flugzeiten: New York - 4 Stunden; Miami - 3 Stunden; Toronto - 4 Stunden; Puerto Rico - 1 Stunde; London - 8 Stunden; Frankfurt - 9 Stunden; Paris - 8 Stunden.

Airlines aus/nach Nordamerika: Air Canada, American Airlines, BWIA, Continental Airlines, US Air.

Airlines aus/nach GB: BWIA, British Airways, Virgin Atlantic und Sunsail Airways mit Verbindungen in übrige Europa.

Airlines von/zu anderen Inseln: LIAT, Air St Kitts/Nevis, Carib Aviation, Caribbean Star Airlines, Montserrat Airways, Caribbean Sun.

ANREISE AUF DEM SEEWEG

Anlegestellen für Kreuzfahrtschiffe befinden sich in St John's Harbour und Heritage Quay im Herzen der Hauptstadt.

FREMDENVERKEHRSBÜROS

Vereinigte Staaten

Antigua and Barbuda Department of Tourism and Trade
25 S.E. 2nd Avenue, Suite 300, Miami, FL 33131

Tel: 305-381-6762. Fax: 305-381-7908
E-Mail: cganuear@bellsouth.net

Antigua and Barbuda Department of Tourism
610 Fifth Avenue, Suite 311, New York, NY 10020

Gebührenfrei: 888-268-4227. Tel: 212-541-4117
Fax: 212-541-4789. E-Mail: info@antigua-barbuda.org

Embassy of Antigua and Barbuda
3216 New Mexico Avenue NW, Washington, DC 20016

Tel: 202 362 5122. Fax: 202 362 5225
E-Mail: embantbar@aol.com

Kanada

Antigua and Barbuda Department of Tourism & Trade
60 St Claire Avenue East, Suite 304, Toronto, Ontario, M4T 1N5

Tel: 416-961-3085. Fax: 416-961-7218
E-Mail: info@antigua-barbuda-ca.com

Großbritannien

Antigua and Barbuda Tourist Office
15 Thayer Street, London, W1U 3JT

Tel: (44) 20 7486 7073. Fax: (44) 20 7486 1466
Website: www.antigua-barbuda.com
E-Mail: antbar@msn.com

Deutschland, Österreich, Schweiz & Nordeuropa

Fremdenverkehrsamt Antigua und Barbuda
Thomasstr. 11, D-61348 Bad Homburg

Tel: 49-6172-21504
Fax: 49-6172-21513

Frankreich

Office du Tourisme D'Antigua et Barbuda
43 Avenue de Friedland, Paris 75008

Tel: 33 (0) 1 53 75 15 71. Fax 33 (0) 1 53 75 15 69

Italien

Dipartimento del Turismo di Antigua e Barbuda
Via Santa Maria alla Porta, 9, 20123 Milan

Tel/Fax: (039) 02 877 983
Tel (für das Reisegewerbe): (039) 02 720 987 27

Antigua und Barbuda

Antigua and Barbuda Department of Tourism
Government Complex, Queen Elizabeth Highway, St John's

Tel: 268-462-0480
Fax: 268-462-2483
E-Mail: deptourism@antigua.gov.ag

Antigua Hotels & Tourists Association
Island House, New Gates Street, P.O. Box 454, St John's

Tel: 268-462-0374. Fax: 268-462-3702
E-Mail: ahta@candw.ag

Antigua e Barbuda: un angolo di paradiso

Della piccola società interconnessa di Antigua e Barbuda si diceva una volta che «se si va sufficientemente indietro nel tempo, sono tutti parenti». Oggi questi parenti sono tornati per una grande rimpatriata. Ai volti tradizionalmente neri, bianchi e arabi della popolazione si mescolano oggi facce brune dalla Repubblica Dominicana.

Secoli fa i nostri nonni e i loro fratelli partirono per Santo Domingo in cerca di opportunità economiche, per tagliare la canna da zucchero. Di molti se ne persero le tracce finché non tornò a casa la loro prole per rivendicare la propria nazionalità. Oggi quindi nell'aula della scuola elementare troviamo Davis seduto davanti a Diaz, e Pena e Peters sono migliori amici.

Al mercato del sabato le donne antiguane comprano verdure dai rivenditori dominicani, fanno una passeggiata in centro per comprare dai negozi libanesi e siriani e poi si rivedono tutte dal parrucchiere spagnolo per farsi l'acconciatura della domenica, portandosi poi a casa un pasto di *chop suey* cinese o di carne di maiale alla giamaicana. Avendo anticipato di molti anni il movimento d'integrazione, questa nazione formata da due isole gemelle di 440 km² è, senza vantarsene, una comunità multinazionale, multietnica e multirazziale.

Tra i nuovi immigranti spagnoli, africani, guyanesi e giamaicani vi sono anche centinaia di americani e europei di carnagione bianca, che oggi superano in numero i discendenti nativi dei mercanti portoghesi e scozzesi, alcuni dei quali vennero, come Colombo, in viaggio di scoperta, e decisero di calare l'ancora qui, spesso nelle pittoresche comunità marinare di English Harbour/Falmouth/Cobbs Cross a sud est, ma sempre di più anche a Jolly Harbour a sud ovest.

La popolazione crescente si è sparsa per tutta l'isola, creando comunità dove una volta esistevano solo campi di canna da zucchero e pascoli per le mucche. I mulini abbandonati – tutto quel che rimane oggi delle piantagioni di zucchero ormai liquidate – sono testimonianze del declino dell'agricoltura e della nascita di altri settori a uso di lavoro meno intensivo, come banche, assicurazioni, telecomunicazioni e aviazione, che hanno contribuito a creare una solida classe media.

Il settore economico principale di Antigua e Barduna rimane tuttavia il turismo. Il settore alberghiero, che comprende hotel esclusivi come Curtain Bluff e alberghi di fama mondiale come Sandals, ma anche centri di villeggiatura a gestione locale come il Jolly Beach Resort (la più grande proprietà del paese) e locande come VIP (sigla inglese di «luoghi molti intimi») soddisfano qualsiasi categoria di visitatore. Rinfrescate dalle brezze marine dei Caraibi, queste isole inondate di sole sono la patria di spiagge tra le più spettacolari del mondo – 365 tesori di sabbia bianca sull'isola di Antigua e luoghi di evasione di sabbia rosa incontaminata a Barbuda. L'isola sorella vanta anche una laguna dall'ambiente incontaminato che ospita una riserva per fregate e una popolazione di daini.

Con un aeroporto internazionale utilizzato da grandi compagnie aeree come American Airlines, Air Canada, British Airways e Virgin Atlantic, oltre alle linee aeree dei Caraibi come BWIA, LIAT e Caribbean Star, raggiungere e partire da Antigua e Barbuda è facile e diretto. Il viaggiatore di affari troverà un sistema di telecomunicazione avanzato - con accesso a Internet in banda larga e collegamenti telefonici internazionali in teleselezione – oltre a strutture per congressi che praticamente trasformano il lavoro in una vacanza.

I passeggeri delle navi crociera approfittano al massimo delle loro tappe per fare acquisti nel porto duty-free della capitale, pranzare negli ottimi ristoranti, visitare i luoghi storici come le rovine di Fort Shirley e Nelson's Dockyard, un museo georgiano restaurato con cantiere navale, fare passeggiate a cavallo, nuotare nelle acque dell'Atlantico con le pastinache o esplorare in kayak le coste del nord est.

Con la crescente ricchezza della popolazione locale si sono sviluppate e diversificate le attività del tempo libero ma alcuni passatempi rimangono pressoché sacri. Gli emigrati di Antigua e Barbuba che vivono all'estero si organizzano per visitare il loro paese di origine nei mesi di luglio e agosto, per coincidere con il Carnevale, che viene definito «il più grande festival estivo dei Caraibi». I festeggiamenti durano undici giorni e Antigua si trasforma in un grande ballo in maschera coloratissimo, animato dalla musica delle steel band, dai canti dolci e/o satirici del calypso e da danze in strada catartiche che spazzano via le differenze tra razze, religioni e ceti sociali.

Anche a Barbuda si svolge nei primi mesi dell'anno un carnevale con programma molto simile, denominato Caribana, e ogni anno per celebrarlo gli abitanti di Antigua si trasferiscono a Barbuda per un fine settimana al gusto di aragosta, granchio, strombo e carne di daino.

Aprile è probabilmente il miglior mese per arrivare in aereo, perché è l'epoca dell'anno in cui si svolge il torneo di cricket e una settimana di gare in barca a vela. Le partite di cricket allo storico parco ricreativo di Antigua sono un autentico festival, dove le vittorie e le sconfitte sono aspetti secondari delle feste che durano tutto il giorno, accompagnate da fiumi di bibite, cibo, musica e risate. È proprio in questo ambiente che sono evidenti l'ospitalità e l'amichevolezza degli antiguani, come testimoniano i fans che ritornano anno dopo anno.

La Sailing Week – una delle regate più famose del mondo – attira gli appassionati della vela e della navigazione da diporto da tutto il mondo, trasformando i porti di English, Falmouth e Jolly in alveari di attività frenetica. Il salone navale primaverile, durante il quale vengono esposte nel porto di Falmouth le imbarcazioni più lussuose del mondo, è una favolosa esperienza, si per chi vuole acquistare che per chi può permettersi solo di ammirare.

"Homecoming," il più recente dei festival, si è svolto per la prima volta durante la giornata dell'indipendenza del 2004. Ha celebrato in particolare l'orgoglio delle comunità locali, le istituzioni e le icone nazionali e gli eventi storici più significativi. Il programma ha compreso anche concorsi di bellezza regionali, una festa di musica gospel e un banchetto di gala con danze. Sulla scia del successo riscontrato dalla manifestazione si prevede che questo festival diventerà un evento annuale.

Gli abitanti di Antigua e Barbuda sono tradizionalmente cristiani e non importa a che ora del mattino si sia conclusa la festa del sabato sera, l'affluenza alla messa di domenica è generalmente molto grande. Benché la città sia dominata dalla cattedrale anglicana di St. John, le chiese metodiste, moraviane, cattoliche, avventiste, battiste, wesleyane, luterane e pentecostali coesistono tranquillamente con altre denominazioni minori come baha'i, islamici e hindu.

Oltre al loro ruolo di protettrici delle anime, le chiese contribuiscono anche alla salvaguardia della cultura. Le fiere gastronomiche anglicane e moraviane, per esempio, sono manifestazioni nazionali nelle quali l'arte culinaria diventa per metà esposizione e per metà consumo. È in questo ambiente che le comunità di immigranti hanno davvero l'occasione di esibirsi, offrendo specialità come sushi giapponese, pollo di montagna dominicano, stufato di capretto di Montserrat, e salsapariglia, un afrodisiaco proveniente da St. Kitts. Naturalmente vi sono anche i piatti preferiti antiguani come il sanguinaccio di riso e maiale e l'alosa con fungie (farina di grano) e le doucana (gnocchetti di farina, patata dolce, cocco e uva passa) con il pesce salato che vanno sempre a ruba.

Queste manifestazioni non vengono organizzate solo per raccogliere fondi per beneficenza, sono anche delle occasioni di autoaffermazione, rassicurandoci che malgrado l'invasione dei valori nordamericani, della TV via cavo e di Internet, siamo ancora abitanti delle Indie Occidentali – nel cuore, nello spirito e nello stomaco.

Antigua e Barbuda – Informazioni generali

Nome: Antigua e Barbuda

Capitale: St John's

Superficie e Posizione: La più grande delle Isole di Sottovento di lingua inglese, Antigua è lunga circa 23 km e larga 18 km, con una superficie di circa 280 km². Il punto più alto è Boggy Peak, che si eleva fino a 402 metri. Barbuda si trova a circa 48 km a nord di Antigua ed è un'isola piatta e corallina con una superficie di circa 176 km².

Antigua e Barbuda si trovano al centro delle Isole di Sottovento, nel Mar dei Caraibi orientale, a circa 17 gradi a nord dell'Equatore. A sud vi sono le isole di Montserrat e Guadeloupe, mentre a nord e a ovest vi sono Nevis, St Kitts, St Barts e St Martin.

Clima: la temperatura oscilla tra 23°C circa in inverno e 30°C circa in estate. La precipitazione annuale è in media di soli 114 cm, il che la rende la più soleggiata delle isole dei Caraibi orientali, con umidità bassa in tutto l'arco dell'anno.

Capo di stato: La regina Elisabetta II, rappresentata dal Governatore Generale Sir James Carlisle

Primo ministro: Baldwin Spencer

Popolazione: 77.000 (NU, 2003)

Lingua: inglese

Valuta: dollaro dei Caraibi orientali (EC$), ma si possono utilizzare anche dollari statunitensi (US$)

Prefisso telefonico internazionale: +1268

Dominio Internet: .ag

Elettricità: in parte dell'isola è di 110 volt, nel resto dell'isola è di 220 volt. La maggior parte degli alberghi offre entrambi i voltaggi.

Banche: Antigua and Barbuda Development Bank, Antigua and Barbuda Investment Bank, Antigua Commercial Bank, Bank of Antigua, Bank of Nova Scotia, First Caribbean International Bank, Global Bank of Commerce, RBTT Bank, Royal Bank of Canada.

Strutture mediche: vi sono un ospedale e una clinica privata, oltre a numerosi medici di famiglia e specialisti. Sono disponibili servizi farmaceutici in tutte le isole.

Passaporti e immigrazion: I cittadini statunitensi, canadesi e dell'UE hanno bisogno di una prova di cittadinanza

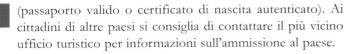

(passaporto valido o certificato di nascita autenticato). Ai cittadini di altre paesi si consiglia di contattare il più vicino ufficio turistico per informazioni sull'ammissione al paese.

ARRIVO IN AEREO

L'aeroporto internazionale V.C. Bird è il punto di entrata per i visitatori che arrivano in volo a Antigua e Barbuda. Vi sono sia voli diretti che coincidenze per l'America del Nord tramite San Juan e St Martin, oltre a vari voli giornalieri per l'Europa. Sono disponibili collegamenti charter e di linea per raggiungere molte delle isole vicine.

Tempi di volo: New York - 4 ore; Miami - 3 ore; Toronto - 4 ore; Puerto Rico - 1 ora; Londra - 8 ore; Francoforte - 9 ore; Parigi - 8 ore.

Linee aeree di collegamento con l'America del Nord: Air Canada, American Airlines, BWIA, Continental Airlines, US Air.

Linee aeree di collegamento con il Regno Unito: BWIA, British Airways, Virgin Atlantic, e Sunsail Airways con coincidenze per l'Europa.

Linee aeree di collegamento tra le isole: LIAT, Air St Kitts/Nevis, Carib Aviation, Caribbean Star Airlines, Montserrat Airways, Caribbean Sun.

ARRIVO VIA MARE

I porti per le navi da crociera sono a St John's Harbour e Heritage Quay, nel cuore della capitale.

UFFICI TURISTICI

Stati Uniti

Antigua and Barbuda Department of Tourism and Trade
25 S.E. 2nd Avenue, Suite 300, Miami, FL 33131

Tel: 305-381-6762. Fax: 305-381-7908
Email: cganuear@bellsouth.net

Antigua and Barbuda Department of Tourism
610 Fifth Avenue, Suite 311, New York, NY 10020

Chiamata gratuita: 888-268-4227
Tel: 212-541-4117. Fax: 212-541-4789
Email: info@antigua-barbuda.org

Ambasciata di Antigua e Barbuda
3216 New Mexico Avenue NW, Washington, DC 20016

Tel: 202 362 5122. Fax: 202 362 5225
Email: embantbar@aol.com

Canada

Antigua and Barbuda Department of Tourism & Trade
60 St Claire Avenue East, Suite 304, Toronto, Ontario, M4T 1N5

Tel: 416-961-3085. Fax: 416-961-7218
Email: info@antigua-barbuda-ca.com

Regno Unito

Antigua and Barbuda Tourist Office
15 Thayer Street, London, W1U 3JT

Tel: (44) 20 7486 7073
Fax: (44) 20 7486 1466
Sito web: www.antigua-barbuda.com
Email: antbar@msn.com

Germania, Austria, Svizzera e Europa del nord

Fremdenverkehrsamt Antigua und Barbuda
Thomasstr. 11, D-61348 Bad Homburg, Germania

Tel: 49-6172-21504
Fax: 49-6172-21513

Francia

Office du Tourisme D'Antigua et Barbuda
43 Avenue de Friedland, Parigi 75008

Tel: 33 (0) 1 53 75 15 71. Fax 33 (0) 1 53 75 15 69

Italia

Dipartimento del Turismo di Antigua e Barbuda
Via Santa Maria alla Porta, 9, 20123 Milano

Tel/Fax: (039) 02 877 983
Tel (per operatori turistici): (039) 02 720 987 27

Antigua e Barbuda

Antigua and Barbuda Department of Tourism
Government Complex, Queen Elizabeth Highway, St John's

Tel: 268-462-0480. Fax: 268-462-2483
Email: deptourism@antigua.gov.ag

Antigua Hotels & Tourists Association
Island House, New Gates Street, P.O. Box 454, St John's

Tel: 268-462-0374. Fax: 268-462-3702
Email: ahta@candw.ag

Antigua y Barbuda: un trocito de paraíso

De la sociedad de Antigua y Barbuda, tan reducida y estrechamente ligada, se solía decir: "Si te remontas lo suficiente en el tiempo, *todo el mundo* está emparentado". Hoy en día, los familiares han vuelto para un gran reencuentro, y las morenas caras de la República Dominicana se mezclan con las de la población tradicional negra, blanca y árabe.

Volvamos a los tiempos en que nuestros abuelos y sus hermanos viajaron a Santo Domingo, buscando mejorar sus economías, para cortar la caña de azúcar. De muchos no se volvió a saber, hasta que sus hijos regresaron a casa para reclamar sus derechos de nacimiento. Y así, en las aulas de las escuelas primarias, Davis se sienta delante de Díaz, y Pena y Peters son amigos inseparables.

En el mercado de los sábados, las mujeres antiguanas compran verduras en los puestos de dominicanos, o caminan hasta las tiendas libanesas y sirias de la ciudad. Más tarde acuden en tropel a las peluquerías hispanas a arreglarse el pelo para el domingo por la mañana, no sin antes recoger una cena preparada de *chop suey* de pollo chino o de cerdo jamaicano al estilo *jerk*.

A años luz del movimiento integrador, esta nación de 274 kilómetros cuadrados y compuesta de dos islas es, sin bombo ni platillo, una comunidad multinacional, multiétnica y multirracial.

Entre los nuevos inmigrantes —hispanos, chinos, africanos, guyaneses y jamaicanos— se cuentan cientos de americanos y europeos blancos, que ya sobrepasan en número a los descendientes nacidos en la isla de mercaderes portugueses y escoceses. Algunos que, como Colón, llegaron en viajes de descubrimiento, optaron por echar el ancla, con frecuencia en las pintorescas comunidades marineras de English Harbour/Falmouth/Cobbs Cross en el sureste y, cada vez más, en Jolly Harbour en el sudoeste.

Esta pujante población se ha expandido por toda la isla, creando comunidades donde antes había cañaverales y pastos para el ganado. Los molinos abandonados —lo único que queda de las desaparecidas fincas de la caña de azúcar— son testimonio del decline de la agricultura y el auge de otras industrias menos laboriosas, como la banca, los seguros, las telecomunicaciones y la aviación, las cuales han contribuido a la consolidación de la clase media.

Sin embargo, el turismo sigue siendo la principal industria de Antigua y Barbuda, y sus numerosos hoteles satisfacen a todos los tipos de visitantes —desde el exclusivo *Curtain Bluff* y el mundialmente famoso *Sandals*, hasta el *Jolly Beach Resort* (gestionado localmente y el mayor bien inmueble del país) y los hospedajes *VIP* (*Very Intimate Places*). Las islas, refrescadas por brisas tropicales y bañadas por el sol,

albergan algunas de las playas más espectaculares del mundo —365 gemas de blancas arenas en Antigua e inmaculados retiros de arenas rosas en Barbuda. La isla hermana también alardea de una laguna ecológica que acoge un santuario bien conservado de pájaros fragata y una población de gamos.

Llegar y salir de Antigua y Barbuda es fácil y directo. Su aeropuerto internacional es utilizado por algunas de las principales líneas aéreas como *American Airlines, Air Canada, British Airways* y *Virgin Atlantic*, además de por otras aerolíneas caribeñas como *BWIA, LIAT* y *Caribbean Star*. Y para el viajero de negocios, las telecomunicaciones avanzadas —incluido Internet de banda ancha y telefonía internacional de marcado directo— y las instalaciones para conferencias, contribuyen a que hacer negocios sea casi una vacación.

Los pasajeros de los cruceros, por otro lado, sacan buen provecho de sus paradas comprando en el puerto libre de impuestos de la capital; comiendo en alguno de sus muchos excelentes restaurantes; explorando lugares históricos como las ruinas de Fort Shirley y Nelson´s Dockyard, un museo y astillero georgiano restaurado; montando a caballo; nadando entre rayas venenosas en el Atlántico; o bordeando la costa nordeste en kayak.

A medida que el nivel de vida de los lugareños ha ido subiendo, las actividades de ocio han aumentado y se han diversificado. Pero algunas fiestas siguen siendo casi sagradas. Los antiguanos y barbudenses que viven en el extranjero planean sus viajes a casa durante julio y agosto para coincidir con el Carnaval, calificado como "el mayor festival veraniego del Caribe". Durante más de once días, Antigua se deleita en una celebración de coloridas máscaras, vigorizante música de bandas de percusión típicas del Caribe, himnos de calipso melodiosos y/o satíricos, y catárticas danzas callejeras que borran de un plumazo las diferencias de raza, fe y clase.

Caribana, el carnaval de Barbuda, tiene una estructura similar y se celebra más temprano. Los antiguanos se trasladan a la isla hermana para celebrarlo y pasar un fin de semana aderezado con una variedad de langosta, cangrejo, concha y venado.

Quizá abril sea el mes con más visitantes, pues se suele celebrar entonces el *Test Cricket* y la Semana de la Vela. El críquet en los históricos *Recreation Grounds* de Antigua es de por sí un festival, y ganar o perder es sólo un acompañamiento de las largas fiestas donde fluyen las libaciones, la comida, la risa y la música. Es aquí donde la famosa hospitalidad y simpatía antiguanas se ponen de mayor manifiesto, como atestiguan los aficionados que vuelven un año detrás de otro.

Por otro lado, la Semana de la Vela –una de las principales regatas del mundo– atrae regatistas y entusiastas de las embarcaciones de todos los lugares del mundo, transformando los puertos de English, Falmouth y Jolly en verdaderos hervideros de actividad. El *Boat Show* de primavera, cuando los barcos más lujosos del mundo se exhiben en Falmouth Harbour, es toda una experiencia para los compradores y los maravillados espectadores.

Homecoming, el más reciente de los festivales, se introdujo en el Día de la Independencia de 2004. La celebración se centró en el orgullo de la comunidad, las instituciones e iconos nacionales y en importantes eventos históricos. También tuvo actividades como concursos de belleza por zonas, un festival de *gospel*, y un banquete y baile de gala. Debido a su éxito, se espera que se convierta en un evento anual.

Los antiguanos y barbudenses son de tradición cristiana, e independientemente de hasta qué horas de la mañana dure la fiesta nocturna del sábado, la asistencia a la iglesia el domingo suele ser masiva. Si bien la catedral anglicana de St John´s domina la ciudad, las iglesias metodista, morava, católica, adventista, baptista, de Wesley, luterana y de Pentecostés conviven pacíficamente con congregaciones más pequeñas como las bahai, musulmana e hindú.

Además de ser las guardianas de las almas, las iglesias juegan su papel a la hora de conservar la cultura. Las ferias de comida anglicana y morava, por ejemplo, son acontecimientos nacionales en los que el arte culinario participa tanto de la exhibición como de la consumición. Es entonces que las comunidades de inmigrantes muestran lo mejor de sí mismas, ofreciendo delicias tan variadas como el *sushi* japonés, el pollo montañero dominicano, el estofado *kiddie* de Montserrat y la zarzaparrilla, un afrodisíaco de los habitantes de St Kitts. Por supuesto, no faltan los preferidos del lugar que, como la morcilla de arroz marinada; el fungie (una mezcla de harina de maíz y kimbombó) con el sábalo, y la doucana (bolas de harina y fruta seca) con salazones de pescado, duran nada y menos.

Estos acontecimientos no sirven sólo para recaudar fondos para las iglesias, sino que son indiscutibles autoafirmaciones, confirmaciones de que, a pesar de la invasión de los valores norteamericanos, la televisión por cable e Internet, aún somos antillanos ahí donde realmente cuenta: en el estómago, el corazón y el espíritu.

Antigua y Barbuda – Datos generales

Nombre: Antigua y Barbuda

Capital: St John's

Tamaño y ubicación: Antigua es la mayor de las Islas Leeward de habla inglesa. Tiene 23 km de largo, 18 km de ancho y un área aproximada de 174 km². Su punto más alto, Boggy Peak, se eleva 402 m. Barbuda está situada a unos 48 km al norte de Antigua y es una isla de coral llana con un área aproximada de 109 km².

Antigua y Barbuda está situada en el centro de las Islas Leeward en el Caribe Oriental, aproximadamente a 17 grados al norte del ecuador. Al sur están las islas de Montserrat y Guadalupe, y al norte y al oeste están Nevis, St Kitts, St Barts y St Martin.

Clima: Las temperaturas varían de alrededor de los 21 grados centígrados en los meses de invierno, a los algo menos de 30 en verano. Las precipitaciones anuales son de un promedio de 114 cm, lo cual la convierte en la más soleada de las islas del Caribe Oriental, con escasa humedad en cualquier época el año.

Jefe de Estado: La reina Isabel II, representada por el gobernador general Sir James Carlisle

Primer Ministro: Baldwin Spencer

Población: 77.000 (ONU, 2003)

Idioma: Inglés

Moneda: Dólar del Caribe Oriental (EC$); también se aceptan dólares estadounidenses (US$)

Código telefónico internacional: +1268

Dominio de internet: .ag

Electricidad: En parte de la isla hay 110 voltios, y en el resto 220. La mayoría de los hoteles tienen los dos voltajes.

Bancos: *Antigua and Barbuda Development Bank, Antigua and Barbuda Investment Bank, Antigua Commercial Bank, Bank of Antigua, Bank of Nova Scotia, First Caribbean International Bank, Global Bank of Commerce, RBTT Bank, Royal Bank of Canada.*

Servicios médicos: Existe un hospital y una clínica privada, así como numerosos médicos de cabecera y especialistas. Hay farmacias por toda la isla.

Pasaportes e inmigración: Los ciudadanos de los EE UU, Canadá y la Unión Europea necesitan prueba de ciudadanía (pasaporte válido o certificado de nacimiento compulsado). Los residentes de otros países deben ponerse en contacto con la oficina de turismo más cercana para conocer los requerimientos de entrada.

VUELOS

El aeropuerto internacional *V.C. Bird* es el punto de entrada para los visitantes que llegan en avión a Antigua y Barbuda. Hay tanto vuelos directos como conexiones con Norteamérica vía San Juan y St Martin, y varios vuelos diarios desde Europa. También hay vuelos regulares y chárter a muchas de las islas vecinas.

Tiempos de vuelo: Nueva York - 4 h; Miami - 3 h; Toronto - 4 h; Puerto Rico - 1 h; Londres - 8 h; Francfort - 9 h; París - 8 h.

Aerolíneas desde Norteamérica: *Air Canada, American Airlines, BWIA, Continental Airlines, US Air.*

Aerolíneas desde el Reino Unido: *BWIA, British Airways, Virgin Atlantic,* y *Sunsail Airways* con conexiones a Europa.

Aerolíneas entre las islas: *LIAT, Air St Kitts/Nevis, Carib Aviation, Caribbean Star Airlines, Montserrat Airways, Caribbean Sun.*

NAVEGACIÓN

Los puertos para los cruceros están situados en St John's Harbour y Heritage Quay, en el corazón de la capital.

OFICINAS DE TURISMO

Estados Unidos

Departamento de Turismo y Comercio de Antigua y Barbuda
25 S.E. 2nd Avenue, Suite 300, Miami, FL 33131

Tfno: 305-381-6762
Fax: 305-381-7908
Email: cganuear@bellsouth.net

Departamento de Turismo de Antigua y Barbuda
610 Fifth Avenue, Suite 311, Nueva York, NY 10020

Número gratuito: 888-268-4227
Tfno: 212-541-4117
Fax: 212-541-4789
Email: info@antigua-barbuda.org

Embajada de Antigua y Barbuda
3216 New Mexico Avenue NW, Washington, DC 20016

Tfno: 202 362 5122. Fax: 202 362 5225
Email: embantbar@aol.com

Canadá

Departamento de Turismo y Comercio de Antigua y Barbuda
60 St Claire Avenue East, Suite 304, Toronto, Ontario, M4T 1N5

Tfno: 416-961-3085. Fax: 416-961-7218
Email: info@antigua-barbuda-ca.com

Reino Unido

Antigua and Barbuda Tourist Office
15 Thayer Street, London, W1U 3JT

Tfno: (44) 20 7486 7073
Fax: (44) 20 7486 1466
Website: www.antigua-barbuda.com
Email: antbar@msn.com

Alemania, Austria, Suiza y Norte de Europa

Fremdenverkehrsamt Antigua und Barbuda
Thomasstr. 11, D-61348 Bad Homburg, Alemania

Tfno: 49-6172-21504. Fax: 49-6172-21513

Francia

Office du Tourisme D'Antigua et Barbuda
43 Avenue de Friedland, París 75008,

Tfno: 33 (0) 1 53 75 15 71. Fax 33 (0) 1 53 75 15 69

Italia

Dipartimento del Turismo di Antigua e Barbuda
Via Santa Maria alla Porta, 9, 20123 Milán,

Tfno/Fax: (039) 02 877 983
Tfno (para viajes de negocios): (039) 02 720 987 27

Antigua y Barbuda

Departamento de Turismo de Antigua y Barbuda
Government Complex, Queen Elizabeth Highway, St John's

Tfno: 268-462-0480. Fax: 268-462-2483
Email: deptourism@antigua.gov.ag

Asociación de Turistas y Hoteles de Antigua
Island House, New Gates Street, P.O. Box 454, St John's

Tfno: 268-462-0374. Fax: 268-462-3702
Email: ahta@candw.ag

J Jones

GOVERNOR-GENERAL

H.E. Sir James Carlisle
Government House
Independence Avenue
St John's, Antigua.
Tel: (268) 462-0003

MINISTERS OF
GOVERNMENT

Hon. W. Baldwin Spencer
Prime Minister & Minister of
Foreign Affairs
Tel: (268) 462-0773

Hon. Justin L. Simon
Attorney General & Minister of
Legal Affairs
Tel: (268) 462-8867

Hon. Willmoth Daniel
Deputy Prime Minister &
Minister of Works,
Transportation & the
Environment
Tel: (268) 462-0890

Dr Hon. L. Errol Cort
Minister of Finance &
Economy
Tel: (268) 462-3588

Hon. Harold E.E. Lovell
Minister of Tourism & Civil
Aviation
Tel: (268) 462-0787

Sen. Hon. Colin Derrick
Minister of Justice
Tel: (268) 462-0017

Hon. Hilson Baptiste
Minister of Housing, Culture &
Social Transformation
Tel: (268) 562-5148

Dr Hon. Jacqui Quinn-Leandro
Minister of Labour, Public
Administration &
Empowerment
Tel: (268) 562-3860

Hon. Bertrand Joseph
Minister of Education
Tel: (268) 462-4959

Hon. John H. Maginley
Minister of Health, Sports &
Youth Affairs
Tel: (268) 562-1675

Hon. Charlesworth T. Samuel
Minister of Agriculture, Lands,
Marine Resources & Agro
Industries
Tel: (268) 462-1007

Sen. Hon. Aziz Hadeed
Minister without Portfolio
Tel: (268) 562-4378

Sen. Hon. Joanne Massiah
Minister of State attached to
the Ministry of Agriculture,
Lands, Marine Resources and
Agro Industry with
responsibility for Marine
Affairs & Food Production
Tel: (268) 562-4679

Hon. Trevor Walker
Minister of State attached to
the Office of the Prime
Minister with responsibility for
Barbuda Affairs
Tel: (268) 562-5029

Sen. Hon. Dr. Edmond
Mansoor
Minister of State attached to
the Office of the Prime
Minister with responsibility for
Information, Broadcasting &
Telecommunications
Tel: (268) 462-8899

Hon. Winston Williams
Minister of State attached to
the Ministry of Health, Sports
& Youth Affairs with
responsibility for Sports &
Youth Affairs
Tel: (268) 462-5522

Hon. Eleston M. Adams
Minister of State attached to
the Ministry of Housing,
Culture & Social
Transformation with
responsibility for Culture
including Independence,
Community Pride &
Homecoming Festivities

Sen. Hon. Lenworth Johnson
Parliamentary Secretary
attached to the Ministry of
Finance & Economy
Tel: (268) 462-4860

ACCOUNTANTS

Allene Thomas & Associates
Upper High Street
St John's
Tel: (268) 562-1871
Fax: (268) 562-1870

CAS Hewlett & Co. Ltd
Hewlett House
Tel: (268) 462-1373
Fax: (268) 462-2268

C D Charles Chartered Accountants
Redcliffe Street
St John's
Tel: (268) 462-2355
Fax: (268) 562-0105
Email: dcharles@candw.ag

Coopers Lybrand
Old Parham Road
St John's
Tel: (268) 462-4071
Fax: (268) 462-3465

Derrick & Watt Accountants
Coolidge
Tel: (268) 462-5525
Fax: (268) 462-5380

Forbes & Associates
High Street
Tel: (268) 460-7917
Fax: (268) 460-9052

Gregory & Associates
Redcliffe Street
St John's
Tel: (268) 462-2355
Fax: (268) 462-2355

KPMG
Sagicor Financial Centre
St John's
Tel: (268) 462-8868
Email: kpmg@kpmg.ag

OAK Consulting Services
William Martin Building
St John's
Tel: (268) 562-4520
Fax: (268) 562-4520

Pannell Kerr Forster
Redcliffe Street
St John's
Tel: (268) 462-0827
Fax: (268) 462-4747

PriceWaterhouseCoopers
Old Parham Road
Tel: (268) 462-3000
Email: pwc@candw.ag

MLC Accounting Services
Lower Newgate Street
St John's
Tel: (268) 462-4533
Fax: (268) 462-4533

Paperworks
Falmouth Main Road
Tel: (268) 560-2372
Email: paperwks@candw.ag

Seamon Accounting Services
Falmouth
Tel: (268) 460-7540

AIR AMBULANCE SERVICES

AAA-Air Ambulance America
Tel: (800) 222-3564
Tel: (512) 479-8000

Aero Ambulance International
Tel: (268) 461-8127

Aero Jet International
San Juan
Puerto Rico
Tel: (787) 724 1694
Fax: (787) 721 0721

Medical Air Services
Nevis Street
Tel: (268) 462-6256
Fax: (268) 463-9225

AIRCRAFT CHARTER

Carib Aviation
V C Bird International Airport
Tel: (268) 481-2400
Fax: (268) 481-2405
Email: caribav@candw.ag

Caribbean Helicopters Ltd
Jolly Harbour
Tel: (268) 460-5900
Fax: (268) 460-5901

Norman Aviation Ltd
V C Bird International Airport
Tel: (268) 462-2445
Fax: (268) 462-2445

AIRLINES

Air Canada
V C Bird International Airport
Tel: (268) 462-1147
Fax: (268) 462-2679

Air Caribes Dca Ltd
V C Bird International Airport
Tel: (268) 462-2523

American Airlines/American Eagle
V C Bird International Airport
Tel: (268) 462-0950
Fax: (268) 462-2067

BWIA West Indies Airways
Woods Mall
St John's
Tel: (268) 480-2912
Fax: (268) 480-2940

British Airways
V C Bird International Airport
Tel: (268) 462-0876
Fax: (268) 462-3218

Carib Aviation
V C Bird International Airport
Tel: (268) 481-2400
Fax: (268) 481-2405
Email: caribav@candw.ag

Caribbean Star Airlines
Airport Road
Tel: (268) 480-2591
Fax: (268) 480-2592
Email:
customerservice@flycaribbeanstar.com

AIRLINES (Cont'd)

Continental Airlines
V C Bird International Airport
Tel: (268) 462-5355

LIAT (1974) Ltd
V C Bird International Airport
Tel: (268) 480-5600
Fax: (268) 480-5635

US Airways
Tel: (800) 622-1015

Virgin Atlantic
V C Bird International Airport
Tel: (268) 560-2079
Fax: (268) 562-1629

APARTMENTS, CONDOMINIUMS, VILLAS & GUESTHOUSES

Amor Villas
Crosbies
Tel: (268) 462-0877
Fax: (268) 462-4674

Antigua Village Condominium
Beach Resort
Dickenson Bay
Tel: (268) 462-2930
Fax: (268) 462-0375

Barrymore Beach Club
Runaway Beach
Tel: (268) 462-4101
Fax: (268) 462-4140

Barrymore Properties
Runaway Bay
Tel: (268) 462-4102

Benjies Villas
Crawl Bay
Tel: (268) 460-4474

Brown's Bay Villas
Browns Bay
Tel: (268) 460-4173
Fax: (268) 460-4175

Coolidge Apartments
Atlantic Avenue
Tel: (268) 460-2914

Coral Sands
Runaway Bay
Tel: (268) 461-0925

Coral Villas
Crosbies
Tel: (268) 461-3278
Fax: (268) 461-3278

Crabbs Cabanas
Crabbs Peninsular
Tel: (268) 461-2113
Fax: (268) 463-3750

Eden Place Apartments/SE Realty
All Saints Road
Tel: (268) 560-4451
Fax: (268) 560-4451

Emerald Cove Ltd.
Nonsuch Bay
Tel: (268) 463-2391
Fax: (268) 463-2373

Fountain Hill Village
Marble Hill
Tel: (268) 461-3239

Hadeed S&E Apartments
Crosbies
Tel: (268) 462-0877
Fax: (268) 462-4674

Harbour View Apartments
Falmouth
Tel: (268) 460-1762

Marble Hill Apartments
Marble Hill
Tel: (268) 461-5557

Maxi Apartments
Factory Road
Tel: (268) 462-2282

Nedds Guest House
Barbuda
Tel: (268) 460-0059

O'Beez Apartments
Factory Road
Tel: (268) 461-4661
Fax: (268) 462-5363

Runaway Beach Club
Runaway
Tel: (268) 462-1318
Fax: (268) 462-4172

Sea Fern Apartments
Hodges Bay
Tel: (268) 560 6242

South Coast Horizons
Cades Bay
Tel: (268) 460-7915
Fax: (268) 463-3177

Time-A-Way Apartments
Runaway Bay
Tel: (268) 462-0775
Fax: (268) 462-2587

Vacation Villas Antigua
Runaway Beach
Tel: (268) 462-4101

Whitegate Cottages & Apartments
Campsite
Tel: (268) 462-1285
Fax: (268) 462-0900

ART GALLERIES & MUSEUMS

Afrikcarib
Heritage Quay
Tel: (268) 562-0280

The Art Gallery
Jolly Harbour
Tel: (268) 562-3987

Calypso Graphics/Gilly Gobinet
Runaway Bay
Tel: (268) 461-0761
Fax: (268) 461-0761

Dockyard Museum
Nelson's Dockyard
Tel: (268) 460-8181

Gomac Art Gallery
St Mary's Street
Tel: (268) 460-7245

Harmony Hall
Near Freetown
Tel: (268) 460-4120

Hide Restaurant & Art Gallery
Mamora Bay
Tel: (268) 460-3666
Fax: (268) 460-3667

Island Arts & The Yoda Guy
Heritage Quay
Tel: (268) 462-2787
Fax: (268) 462-1480

Kate Design
Redcliffe Quay
Tel: (268) 460-5971
Fax: (268) 460-5972/3

Museum of Antigua & Barbuda
Long Street
Tel: (268) 462-1469/462-4930

2000 Millennium Art Gallery & Gift
Shop
Jolly Harbour
Tel: (268) 562-3987

Rhythm of Blue Art Gallery
Dockyard Drive
Tel: (268) 562-2230

AUTOMOBILE DEALERS

Ace Enterprises Ltd
Tomlinson's
Tel: (268) 462-1289
Fax: (268) 462-1290
Email: harneymo@candw.ag

Antigua Motors (1993) Ltd
Old Parham Road
Tel: (268) 462-3234
Fax: (268) 462-0395

Hadeed Motors
Old Parham Road
Tel: (268) 481-2500
Fax: (268) 481-2525
Email: hadeedmotors@yahoo.com

Harney Motors Ltd
Factory & American Roads
Tel: (268) 462-1062
Fax: (268) 462-1024
harneymo@candw.ag

Ideal Autos Ltd
Cassada Gardens
Tel: (268) 462-3339
Fax: (268) 462-3341

Island Motors Ltd
Queen Elizabeth Highway
Tel: (268) 462-2199
Fax: (268) 462-2138

Shaw Brothers Enterprises
Fort Road
Tel: (268) 462-4981
Fax: (268) 462-4981

AVIATION

V C Bird International Airport
Main Office
Tel: (268) 462-3082
Air Traffic Control
Tel: (268) 562-0302
Fire Station
Tel: (268) 462-3062/63
Security Division
Tel: (268) 462-4670
Meteorological Services
Tel: (268) 462-0930
Fax: (268) 462-4606
VIP Lounge
Tel: (268) 462-4605

BANKS

American International Bank
Friars Hill Road
St John's
Tel: (268) 462-3243
Fax: (268) 462-6675

American Pacific Trading
Newgate Street
St John's
Tel: (268) 462-8000
Fax: (268) 462-9898

Antigua & Barbuda Development Bank
St Mary's Street
St John's
Tel: (268) 462-0838
Fax: (268) 462-0839

Antigua & Barbuda Investment
Bank Ltd
Redcliffe Street
St John's
Tel: (268) 480-2700
Fax: (268) 480-2850
Email: abib@abifinancial.com

Antigua Commercial Bank
St Mary's Street
St John's
Tel: (268) 481-4200
Fax: (268) 481-4280

Antigua Overseas Bank Ltd
High Street, St John's
Tel: (268) 480-2700
Fax: (268) 480-2750
Email: aob@abifinancial.com

Bank of Antigua
Airport Boulevard
Tel: (268) 480-5300
Fax: (268) 480-5433

Bank of Europe
Independence Drive
St John's
Tel: (268) 562-4274

Bank of Nova Scotia
High Street
St John's
Tel: (268) 480-1500
Fax: (268) 480-1554

Barrington Bank
Woods Centre
St John's
Tel: (268) 481-1777
Fax: (268) 481-1778
Email: common@barrington.ag

BANKS (Cont'd)

Caribbean American Bank
Woods Centre
St John's
Tel: (268) 462-9210 / 9235

East Caribbean Central Bank
Factory Road, St John's
Tel: (268) 462-2489
Fax: (268) 462-2490

Eurofed Bank
High Street, St John's
Tel: (268) 460-5451
Fax: (268) 460-5455

Fidelity International Bank
Woods Centre, St John's
Tel: (268) 460-7546

Financial Service Group
Woods Centre
St John's
Tel: (268) 462-9214
Fax: (268) 462-9215

First Caribbean International Bank
(Barbados) Ltd
High Street
St John's
Tel: (268) 480-5000
Fax: (268) 462-4910

Global Bank of Commerce
Woods Centre
St John's
Tel: (268) 480-2240
Fax: (268) 462-1831
Email: customerservice@gbc.ag

Hanover Bank
Fax: (268) 462-9215

International Management & Trust
Services Antigua
Tel: (268) 462-9511

Meinl Bank Antigua
High Street
St John's
Tel: (268) 460-5700
Fax: (268) 460-5755

Overseas Development Trust
Corporation
Woods Centre
St John's
Tel: (268) 462-9232
Fax: (268) 462-9215

RBTT Bank Ltd
High Street
St John's
Tel: (268) 462-4217
Fax: (268) 462-5040

Royal Bank of Canada
High & Market Streets
St John's
Tel: (268) 480-1150
Fax: (268) 480-1190

Stanford International Bank Ltd
Pavilion Drive
Coolidge
Tel: (268) 480-3700
Fax: (268) 480-3737
Email: sibprivate@stanfordeagle.com

Swiss American Bank Ltd
Friars Hill Road
St John's
Tel: (268) 480-2230
Fax: (268) 462-1831

VTI Bank Ltd
Jardines Court
St John's
Tel: (268) 460-7385

Worldwide International Bank Ltd
Market Street
St John's
Tel: (268) 462-9511

BIKES & SCOOTER RENTAL

JT's Rent-A-Scoot
Tel: (268) 774-1905

Paradise Boat Sales
Tel: (268) 460-7125

Sun Cycles Bicycle Rental
Hodges Bay
Tel: (268) 461-0324

Shipwreck Rent-A-Scooter
Dockyard Drive
Tel: (268) 460-6087

Tropical Rentals
Tel: (268) 562-5180

BOAT RENTALS & CHARTERS

Antigua Charter Services
Nelson's Dockyard
Tel: (268) 460-2615
Fax: (268) 460-2616

Caribbean Development Antigua Ltd
Jolly Harbour
Tel: (268) 462-7686

Caribbean Water Sport Sail
Tel: (268) 462-7245

Cay Heaven Charters
All Saints
Tel: (268) 462-0834

Coral Ark Love Boat
Redcliffe Street
Tel: (268) 462-9731

Jolly Roger (Antigua) Ltd
Redcliffe Street
St John's
Tel: (268) 480-1225
Fax: (268) 462-2065
Email: tropad@candw.ag

Kokomo Cat Cruises
Jolly Harbour
Tel: (268) 462-7245
Fax: (268) 462-8305

Miguel's Holiday Adventure
Villa
Tel: (268) 461-0361

Paradise Boat Sales
Tel: (268) 460-7125
Fax: (268) 462-6276
Email: paradise@candw.ag

Sun Yacht Charters
Nelson's Dockyard
Tel: (268) 460-2615
Fax: (268) 460-2616

Sunsail
Nelson's Dockyard
Tel: (268) 463-6224
Fax: (268) 460-2616
Email: charterservices@candw.ag

Treasure Island Cruises
Five Islands
Tel: (268) 461-8675
Fax: (268) 461-8698
Email: armstronge@candw.ag

Wadadli Cats
Redcliffe Quay
Tel: (268) 562-1803
Fax: (268) 462-3661

BOOKSHOPS

Adventist Book Centre
Nevis Street
Tel: (268) 462 4546

Best of Books
Benjie's Mall
Lower Redcliffe Street
Box 433
St John's
Tel: (268) 562 3198
Fax: (268) 462 2199
Email: bestofbooks@yahoo.com

Caribbean Educational Services Ltd
St Mary's Street
St John's
Tel: (268) 462 3993
Fax: (268) 462 3995

Christian Bookshop
Newgate Lane, St John's
Tel: (268) 462 9464
Fax: (268) 463 5474

Christian Literature Centre
Lower Church Street
St John's
Tel: (268) 462 2024
Fax: (268) 462 2023

Frame-it (1991) Ltd
St Mary's Street
St John's
Tel: (268) 462 3993
Fax: (268) 462 3995

G & L Bookshop
St Mary's Street
St John's
Tel: (268) 460 5504
Fax: (268) 462 1884

Island Newstand
Bob Camacho's Arcade
Lower High Street
St John's
Tel: (268) 462 2457
Fax: (268) 462 2458

Lord Jim's Locker
Antigua Yacht Club Marina
English Harbour
Tel: (268) 460 1147
Fax: (268) 560 4093

Map Shop, The
St Mary's Street
St John's
Tel: (268) 462 3993
Fax: (268) 462 3995

PC's Book Review
Corner of St Mary's Street
St John's
Tel: (268) 462 1545

Seventh Day Adventist Book Centre
Tanner Street, St John's
Tel: (268) 462 4546

Stermat Bookstore
1b Newgate Lane
St John's
Tel: (268) 462 0018
Fax: (268) 462 1058

CAR RENTAL

ATS Car Rental & Limousine
Service
Powell's
Tel: (268) 562-1709
Fax: (268) 461-5700
Email: ats@candw.ag

Avis Rent-A-Car
Powell's Estate
Tel: (268) 462-2840
Fax: (268) 462-2848

Budget Rent A Car
Cassada Gardens
Tel: (268) 462-3009
Fax: (268) 460-9177

Capital Car Rentals
Gambles Terrace
Tel: (268) 462-0863

Carters Rent A Car
V C Bird International Airport
Tel: 463-0675

Coleds Car Rental & Leasing
Gambles Terrace
Tel: (268) 462-0464
Fax: (268) 462-0464
Email: coleds@hotmail.com

Dions Rent A Car & Tax Service
V C Bird International Airport
Tel: (268) 462-3466
Fax: (268) 461-3267

Dollar Rent A Car
Factory Road
Tel: (268) 462-0362
Fax: (268) 462-5907
Email: dollarantigua@hotmail.com

Hertz Rent A Car
Carlisle Estate
Tel: (268) 481-4440
Fax: (268) 481-4460
Email: hertz@candw.ag

Huntley Car Rental
Alfred Peters Street
Tel: (268) 462-1575

Hyatt Rent A Car
English Harbour
Tel: (268) 4+0-6551

Ivor's Taxi
Liberta Village
Tel: (268) 460-1241

Jacobs Rent A Car
V C Bird International Airport
Tel: (268) 462-0576

Jeeps 'r' Us Rentals
Tindale Road
Tel: (268) 462-9099

Jonas Rent A Car
Factory Road
Tel: (268) 462-3760
Fax: (268) 463-7625

Lions Car Rental
Airport Road
Tel: (268) 460-1400
Fax: (268) 460-2707

National Car Rental
Fax: (268) 462-2113

Oakland Rent A Car
V C Bird International Airport
Tel: (268) 462-3021

Paradise Car Rentals
Rex Halcyon Cove
Tel: (268) 462-9780

Pats Rent A Car
Crosbies
Tel: (268) 462-6739

Prince's Rent A Car
Fort Road
Tel: (268) 462-0766

Rawlins Supreme Car Rental
St Johnston's Village
Tel: (268) 461-0110
Fax: (268) 461-1878

Richards Rent A Car
V C Bird International Airport
Tel: (268) 462-0976

St John's Car Rental
Branch Avenue
Tel: (268) 462-0594
Fax: (268) 462-6147

Slane's Supreme Car
Lower Newgate Street
Tel: (268) 462-8789

Sted Rent A Car
Airport Road
Tel: (268) 462-9970
Fax: (2680 460-5603

Thrifty Car Rental
Airport Road
Tel: (268) 462-9532
Fax: (268) 463-9030

Tropical Rentals
Tel: (268) 562-5180

Village Car Rental
Anchorage Road
Tel: (268) 461-3746

CLUBS & ASSOCIATIONS

Antigua & Barbuda Bee-Keepers'
Association
Belmont
Tel: (268) 562-2983

Antigua & Barbuda Vendors'
Association
Tanner Street
Tel: (268) 462-5482

Antigua Barbuda Cruise Tourism
Association
8 Redcliffe Quay
Tel: (268) 562-1746
Fax: (268) 562-2858

Antigua Barbuda Union of Teachers
Factory Road
Tel: (268) 462-3750

Antigua & Barbuda Olympic
Association
Redcliffe Street
St John's
Tel: (268) 462-3476
Fax: (268) 462-4811
Email: aboa@candw.ag

Antigua & Barbuda Public Service
Association (ABPS)
All Saints Road
Tel: (268) 461-5821

Antigua & Barbuda Red Cross
Old Parham Road
Tel: (268) 462-0800
Fax: (268) 462-0800

Antigua & Barbuda Sickle Cell
Association
Newgate Lane
Tel: (268) 460-9555

Antigua & Barbuda Stroke Patient
Association
All Saints Road
Tel: (268) 562-0911

Antigua Baptist Association
Redcliffe Street
Tel: (268) 462-1254

Antigua Calypso Enterprise
Falmouth
Tel: (268) 462-8845

Antigua Chamber of Commerce
Popeshead Street
Tel: (268) 462-0743

Antigua Contract Bridge Association
Factory Road
Tel: (268) 462-6393

Antigua Cricket Association
Antigua Recreation Grounds
Tel: (268) 462-9089
Fax: (268) 462-9090

Antigua Employers' Federation
Upper High Street
Tel: (268) 462-0449

Antigua Football Association
Newgate Street
Tel: (268) 480-3232

Antigua Junior Chambers
Old Parham Road
Tel: (268) 462-4979

Antigua Planned Parenthood
Association
Bishopgate Street
Tel: (268) 4462-0947

Antigua Trades & Labour Union
46 North Street
Tel: (268) 462-0090

Antigua Workers' Union
Newgate Street
Tel: (268) 462-2005
Fax: (268) 462-5220

Antigua Yacht Charters
English Harbour
Tel: (268) 463-7101

Antigua Yacht Club
English Harbour
Tel: (268) 460-1799

Caribbean Council for the Blind
All Saints Road
Tel: (268) 462-4111

Employers' Federation
#7 Redcliffe Quay
Tel: (268) 462-0449

Environmental Awareness Group
Long Street
Tel: (268) 462-6236
Fax: (268) 462-6236

Lions Club of Antigua
Cross Street
Tel: (268) 462-0665

Rotary Club of Antigua & Barbuda
P.O. Box 1091
Tel: (268) 462-5760
Fax: (268) 462-0395

CONFERENCE FACILITIES

Antigua Commercial Bank
St Mary's Street
Tel: (268) 481-4200
Fax: (268) 481-4280

City View Hotel
Newgate Street
Tel: (268) 562-1211
Fax: (268) 562-0242

Cortsland Hotel
Upper Gambles
Tel: (268) 462-1395

Heritage Hotel
Heritage Quay
Tel: (268) 462-1247
Fax: (268) 462-1179

Jolly Beach Resort
Bolans Village
Tel: (268) 462-0061
Fax: (268) 562-2302
Email: info@jollybeachresort.com

Multi-purpose Cultural Centre
Perry Bay
Tel: (268) 460-7388

Rex Halcyon Cove Hotel
Dickenson Bay
Tel: (268) 462-0256
Fax: (268) 462-0271

Royal Antiguan Resort
Deep Bay
Tel: (268) 462-3733
Fax: (268) 462-3732

Sandals Antigua Resort & Spa
Dickenson Bay
Tel: (268) 462-0267
Fax: (268) 462-4135

Tradewinds Hotel
Dickenson Bay
Tel: (268) 462-1223
Fax: (268) 462-5007

CUSTOMS

Customs Department
Main Office
Long Street
    Tel: (268) 462-0026
    Fax: (268) 462-2767
Barbuda
    Tel: (268) 460-0085
Coolidge Cargo
    Tel: (268) 462-3160
Crabbs
    Tel: (268) 463-2372
Deep Water Harbour
    Tel: (268) 462-0814
Dockyard
    Tel: (268) 460-1397
Heritage Quay
    Tel: (268) 462-6656
Jolly Harbour
    Tel: (268) 462-7929
Redcliffe Quay
    Tel: (268) 562-1577
V C Bird International Baggage
    Tel: (268) 462-3092
Departure Tax
    Tel: (268) 562-4394

DOCTORS

Dr Dane Abbott
Obstetrician/Gynecologist
Women's Clinic
Tel: (268) 462-4133
Fax: (268) 462-4134

Antigua Optical Co Ltd
Stapleton Lane Clinic
Tel: (268) 462-0031
Fax: (268) 462-0031

Dr Jason Belizaire
Internal Medicine
Woods Centre
Tel: (268) 562-1168
Fax: (268) 562-1200

Dr Philmore Benjamin, MD, Dip
Pharm
Vivian Richards Street
Tel: (268) 462-3630
Fax: (268) 462-3630

Dr Jillia Bird - Optometrist
Milburn House
Tel: (268) 462-1513
Fax: (268) 462-5622

DOCTORS (Cont'd)

Dr Salah Bittar
Lower Nevis Street
Tel: (268) 462-1706
Fax: (268) 462-1706

Dr Carrick-Fraser, Dip Geriatrics
Alpha Building
Tel: (268) 462-1975
Fax: (268) 460-5258

Dr Kelvin P. Charles
Long Street
Tel: (268) 462-4973

Dr Chen
Browne's Avenue
Tel: (268) 560-2368

Dr Delrose Christian
Market & Tanner Streets
Tel: (268) 462-5752
Fax: (268) 462-5752

Dr Ronnie Cooper
Visiting Dermatologist
Ramco Building
Tel: (268) 462-6241
Email: ronniecooper@hotmail.com

Dr Raymond Daoud
St John's Street
Tel: (268) 462-6149
Fax: (268) 460-8584

Dr Alvin Edwards
Upper Redcliffe Street
St John's
Tel: (268) 462-2748
Fax: (268) 462-1976

Dr Gwendolyn Fevrier-Roberts
Obstetrician/Gynecologist
Ramco Building
Tel: (268) 462-2770
Fax: (268) 462-1805

Dr Nicholas Fuller
Long Street
Tel: (268) 462-0391

Dr Edda Hadeed
Pediatrician & Neonatologist
Gambles Medical Centre
Tel: (268) 462-9499
Fax: (268) 461-4282

Dr Elijah James
Newfield Village
Tel: (268) 562-1885
Fax: (268) 562-1884

Dr Joseph John
Surgeon
Medical Surgical Associates
Tel: (268) 562-1169
Fax: (268) 562-3300

Dr Marlene Joseph
Family Physician
Independence Drive
Tel: (268) 462-0542

Dr Frances Kelsick
Obstetrician/Gynecologist
Women's Clinic
Tel: (268) 462-4133
Fax: (268) 462-4134

Dr Sam Kiwomya
Temple & Tanner Street
Tel: (268) 462-2990

Dr Linda Lovell-Roberts
Paediatrician
2nd Avenue Gambles
Tel: (268) 462-3710
Fax: (268) 462-3105

Dr Edmond Mansoor
Market & Tanner Streets
Tel: (268) 462-4634
Fax: (268) 462-2633

Dr Rose Massiah
Family Physician
41 Church Street
Tel: (268) 562-2833
Fax: (268) 562-2784

Dr Fouad Naffouj
Dollar Building
Tel: (268) 562-1620
Fax: (268) 462-9443

Dr Bertrand O'Marde
Surgeon
Ramco Building
Tel: (268) 462-1935
Fax: (268) 462-1835

Ortho Medical Associates
Woods Centre
St John's
Tel: (268) 460-7720
Fax: (268) 461-8065

Dr P Raj
Ramco Building
Tel: (268) 462-6241

Dr George Roberts
ENT and Head & Neck Surgeon
Ramco Building
Tel: (268) 462-2770
Fax: (268) 462-1805

Dr Raymond Rogers
Stapleton Lane Clinic
Tel: (268) 462-0031
Fax: (268) 462-0031

Dr Soumitra SenGupta
Temple Street
Tel: (268) 462-1467

Dr K K Singh
Orthopaedic Surgeon
Ortho Medical Associates
Woods Centre
St John's
Tel: (268) 462-1932
Fax: (268) 461-8065

Dr Nidhi Singh
Family Physician – Specialists in
Addiction
Ortho Medical Associates
Woods Centre
St John's
Tel: (268) 460-7720
Fax: (268) 461-8065

Dr Arlene Sorhaindo
Pediatrician
Stapleton Lane
Tel: (268) 562-1931
Fax: (268) 562-1931

Dr Ian C Walwyn
Ophthalmologist
Stapleton Lane
Tel: (268) 562-1931
Fax: (268) 562-1931

Dr R A Walwyn
Ophthalmologist
Tel: (268) 462-0031
Fax: (268) 462-0031

Dr Andre Winter
Obstetrician/Gynecologist
Tel: (268) 562-1977
Fax: (268) 562-1978

DENTISTS

A A-Antigua Barbuda Dental Group
Newgate Street
St Jon's
Tel: (268) 460-3368
Fax: (268) 462-2777

Dr Bernard Evan-Wong
Gambles Medical Centre
Tel: (268) 462-3050
Fax: (268) 463-9601

Dr B K Wassouf
Family Dentist
Dollar Building
Tel: (268) 462-9443

Family Dentistry
Cross & Newgate Streets
Tel: (268) 462-0058
Fax: (268) 462-2777

Dr Maxwell Francis
Cross & Newgate Streets
Tel: (268) 462-0058
Fax: (268) 462-2777

Gentle Dental Services
High Street
Tel: (268) 462-2000
Fax: (268) 460-7276

Dr Jamil Hadeed
Lower All Saints Road
Tel: (268) 462-2820

Dr Derek Marshall & Associate-
Dental Care Clinic
Ramco Building
Tel: (268) 462-2525
Fax: (268) 462-2553

Dr S V Raj
Bishop Lodge Building
Tel: (268) 461-6810
Fax: (268) 461-6810

Dr Sengupta & Associates
Woods Centre
Tel: (268) 462-9312
Fax: (268) 462-9314

Seventh Day Adventist Dental Clinic
Nevis Street
Tel: (268) 462-9393
Fax: (268) 462-9633

Williams & Associates Dental Clinic
28 Long Street
Tel: (268) 462-1381
Fax: (268) 460-6300

EDUCATION

Antigua & Barbuda Hospitality and
Training Institute
Dutchman's Bay
Tel: (268) 462-3066
Fax: (268) 462-8782

Antigua & Barbuda International
Institute of Technology
Tel: (268) 480-2400
Fax: (268) 480-2411

Antigua State College
Golden Grove
Tel: (268) 462-0613

Caribbean Centre Sports Education
& Training
Blue Waters
Tel: (268) 463-8504

Cornwall International College
Gunthropes
Tel: (268) 462-6148

National College of Martial Arts
Ottos
Tel: (268) 461-2638

The Director of Vocational
Education
Factory Road
Tel: (268) 460-7581

Rastafari Livity Institute
Cassada Gardens
Tel: (268) 560-4393
Fax: (268) 560-4393

University of Health Sciences
Antigua
Dowhill Campus
Tel: (268) 460-1391
Fax: (268) 460-1477

Antigua & Barbuda Technical
Vocational Centre
Tel: (268) 462-2935

Deb'Onair Enterprises
Upper St Mary's Street
Tel: (268) 462-0366
Fax: (268) 560-2165

Institute of Business Education &
Training
A S F Gunthropes
Tel: (268) 462-7933

Technical & Vocational Training
Centre
Nugent Area
Tel: (268) 462-7923

University of the West Indies
Factory Road
Tel: (268) 562-2571
Fax: (268) 462-2968

EMERGENCY SERVICES

AMBULANCE 911
FIRE   911
POLICE   911 or 777

Fire
(268) 462-0044

Hospital
(268) 462-0251

Police
(268) 462-0125

Office of Disaster Preparedness
(268) 462-4402

Alcoholics Anonymous (AA)
(268) 463-3155

Air/Sea Rescue
(268) 462-3062

Ambulance
(268) 462-0251

Domestic Violence
(268) 463-5555

Friends Hotline
800-4357(HELP)

FERRY SERVICES

Barbuda Ferry Service
c/o D & J Forwarders & Tours
Tel: (268) 773-9766

Montserrat Ferry Service Opale
Express
c/o Jenny's Tours
Tel: (268) 461-9361
Cell: (268) 464-4188
Email: burkeb@candw.ag

FUNERAL HOMES

Barnes Funeral Home
Newgate Street
Tel: (268) 462-1037

Straffie's Funeral Home
St John's Street
Tel: (268) 462-0575
Fax: (268) 462-0574

FINANCIAL & INVESTMENT

Finance & Development Co Ltd
Old Parham Road
Tel: (268) 481-2569
Fax: (268) 481-2571

Financial Services Corp
Tel: (268) 463-2265
Fax: (268) 462-3330

International Investment &
Commerce Co
Fax: (268) 462-3330

National Mortgage & Trust Co Ltd
Upper High Street
St John's
Tel: (268) 462-9497
Fax: (268) 462-9496
Email: mortgtrust@candw.ag

Stanford Financial Group Ltd
Tel: (268) 480-5900
Fax: (268) 480-5909

HIKING

Historical Awareness Group
Tel: (268) 462-4930/1469

Environmental Awareness Group
Tel: (268) 462-6236

Antigua Hash House Harriers
Tel: (268) 461-0686

HORSEBACK RIDING

Spring Hill Riding Club
Falmouth
Tel: (268) 460-7787 / 773-3139

HOSPITALS & MEDICAL CENTRES

Holberton Hospital
Queen Elizabeth Highway
Tel: (268) 462-0251/2/3/4
Fax: (268) 462-4067

Adelin Medical Centre Ltd
Fort Road
Tel: (268) 462-0866
Fax: (268) 462-2386

HOTELS & RESORTS

Antigua Hotels & Tourist Association
Lower Newgate Street
Tel: (268) 462-0374
Fax: (268) 462-3702
Email: ahta@candw.ag

Admirals Inn
Nelson's Dockyard
Tel: (268) 460-1027
Fax: (268) 460-1534
Email: admirals@candw.ag

Airport Hotel
Airport Road
Tel: (268) 462-1191
Fax: (268) 462-1534

Allegro Resort
Pineapple Beach
Tel: (268) 463-2006
Fax: (268) 463-2452
Email: info@antigua.allegroresorts

Anchorage Inn
McKinnons
Tel: (268) 462-4065
Fax: (268) 462-4066

Amaryllis Hotel
Airport Road
Tel: (268) 462-8690
Fax: (268) 8691

Antigua Village Condo Beach
Resort
Dickenson Bay
Tel: (268) 462-2930
Fax: (268) 462-0375
Email: antiguavillage@candw.ag

Antigua Beachcomber Hotel
Winthropes Bay
Tel: (268) 462-3100
Fax: (268) 462-4012
Email: beachcom@candw.ag

Blue Waters Antigua
Blue Waters
Tel: (268) 462-0290
Fax: (268) 462-0293
Email: bluewaters@candw.ag

Carlisle Bay Club
Old Road Village
Tel: (268) 462-1377
Fax: (268) 462-1365

Catamaran Hotel & Marina
Falmouth Harbour
Tel: (268) 460-1036
Fax: (268) 460-1506

Chez Pascal French Restaurant &
Deluxe Rooms
Galley Bay
Tel: (268) 462-3232
Fax: (268) 460-5730

City View Hotel & Restaurant
Newgate Street
St John's
Tel: (268) 562-1211
Fax: (268) 562-0242

Coco Point Lodge
Codrington
Barbuda
Tel: (268) 462-3816
Fax: (268) 462-5340

Cocobay Resort
Valley Church
Tel: (268) 562-2400
Fax: (268) 562-2424
Email: cocobay@candw.ag

Cocos
Valley Road
Tel: (268) 462-9700
Fax: (268) 462-9423
Email: cocos@candw.ag

Coconut Beach Club
Yeptons Estate
Tel: (268) 462-2520
Fax: (268) 462-3240
coconutbeachclub@reservations.com

Copper & Lumber Store Hotel
Nelson's Dockyard
Tel: (268) 460-1058
Fax: (268) 460-1529

Cortsland Hotel
Upper Gambles
Tel: (268) 462-1395
Fax: (268) 462-1699

Country Inn Cottages
Cobbs Cross
Tel: (268) 460-1469
Fax: (268) 460-1469
Email: inn@candw.ag

Curtain Bluff Hotel
Old Road
Tel: (268) 462-8400
Fax: (268) 462-8409
Email: curtainbluff@candw.ag

Dickenson Bay Cottages
Tel: (268) 462-4940
Fax: (268) 462-4941

Dian Bay Resort & Spa
Dian Bay
Tel: (268) 460-6646
Fax; (268) 460-4400
Email: dianbay@candw.ag

Dove Cove
Dry Hill
Tel: (268) 463-8600
Fax: (268) 463-8601
Email: dovecove@candw.ag

Galleon Beach Club
English Harbour
Tel: (268) 460-1024
Fax: (268) 460-1450
Email: galleonbeach@candw.ag

Galley Bay Resort
Five Islands
Tel: (268) 462-0302
Fax: (268) 462-4551
Email: reservations@antigua-
resorts.com

Grand Royal Antiguan
Deep Bay
Tel: (268) 462-3733
Fax: (268) 462-3732
Email: admin@grandroyalantiguan.com

Harbour View Hotel
Dockyard
Tel: (268) 463-1026

HBK Villa Rentals
Jolly Harbour
Tel: (268) 462-6166 / 67
Email: jollyhbr@candw.ag

Hawksbill Beach Resort
Five Islands
Tel: (268) 462-0301
Fax: (268) 462-1515
Email: hawksbill@candw.ag

Heritage Hotel
Heritage Quay
Tel: (268) 462-1247
Fax: (268) 462-1179
Email: heritagehotel@candw.ag

Joemikes Downtown Hotel Plaza
Nevis Street
Tel: (268) 462-1142
Fax: (268) 462-6056
Email: joemikes@candw.ag

Jolly Beach Resort
Bolans Village
Tel: (268) 462-0061
Fax: (268) 562-2302
Email: info@jollybeachresort.com

Jolly Castle Hotel
Jolly Harbour
Tel: (268) 463-9001
Fax: (268) 462-9033

Jolly Harbour Villas
Jolly Harbour
Tel: (268) 462-7771/2/3
Fax: (268) 462-4900
Email:
hkupin@jollyharbourantigua.com

HOTELS & RESORTS (Cont'd)

Jumby Bay Resort
Jumby Bay Island
Tel: (268) 462-6000
Fax: (268) 462-6020
Email: jumby@candw.ag

K Club
Barbuda
Tel: (268) 460-0300
Fax: (268) 460-0305
Email: kclubbarbuda@candw.ag

Long Bay Hotel
Long Bay
Tel: (268) 463-2005
Fax: (268) 463-2439
Email: longbay@candw.ag

Lord Nelson Beach Hotel
Dutchman's Bay
Tel: (268) 462-3094
Fax: (268) 462-3094

Marina Bay Resort
Dickenson Bay
Tel: (268) 462-3254/58
Fax: (268) 462-2151
Email: marinabay@candw.ag

Ocean Inn
English Harbour
Tel: (268) 460-1263
Fax: (268) 463-7950
Email: oceaninn@candw.ag

Pelican Isle
Johnson's Point
Tel: (268) 462-8385
Fax: (268) 462-4361
Email: pelican@candw.ag

Rex Blue Heron
Johnsons Point
Tel: (268) 462-8564
Fax: (268) 462-8005

Rex Halcyon Cove
Dickenson Bay
Tel: (268) 462-0256
Fax: (268) 462-0271
Email: rexhalcyon@candw.ag

St James's Club
Mamora Bay
Tel: (268) 460-0500
Fax: (268) 460-3015
Email:
reservations@antigua-resorts.com

Sandals Antigua Resort & Spa
Dickenson Bay
Tel: (268) 462-0267
Fax: (268) 462-4135
Email: sandals@candw.ag

Sandpiper Reef Resort
Crosbies
Tel: (268) 462-0939
Fax: (268) 462-1743
Email: sandpiper@candw.ag

Siboney Beach Club
Dickenson Bay
Tel: (268) 462-0806
Fax: (268) 462-3356
Email: siboney@candw.ag

Sunsail Club Colonna
Hodges Bay
Tel: (268) 462-6263
Fax: (268) 462-6430
Email: colonna@candw.ag

The Beach House Barbuda
Palmetto Point, Barbuda
Tel: (268) 725-4042
Fax: (212) 202 3939
Email:
info@thebeachhousebarbuda.com

The Inn at English Harbour
English Harbour
Tel: (268) 460-1014
Fax: (268) 460-1603
Email: theinn@candw.ag

Three Martini Beach Bar Restaurant
& Apartments
Crabbe Hill
Tel: (268) 460-9306
Fax: (268) 481-1735

Tradewinds Hotel
Dickenson Bay
Tel: (268) 462-1223
Fax: (268) 462-5007
Email: twhotel@candw.ag

Willowby Heights Apartments
St Philip's Village
Tel: (268) 460-4105
Fax: (268) 560-9738

IMMIGRATION

Immigration Department
General Office
Queen Elizabeth Highway
    Tel: (268) 562-1387
    Fax: (268) 562-1388
Crabbs
    Tel: (268) 463-3912
Deep Water Harbour
    Tel: (268) 462-9483
Dockyard
    Tel: (268) 463-9410
Heritage Quay
    Tel: (268) 462-7932
Jolly Harbour
    Tel: (268) 462-3590

LAWYERS / ATTORNEYS

Clement Bird
St Mary's Street
Tel: (268) 462-5883
Fax: (268) 462-0077
Email: birdc@candw.ag

Rika Bird & Associates
Long Street
Tel: (268) 562-1880
Fax: (268) 562-1882
Email: birdr@candw.ag

Bowen & Bowen
Dollar Building
Tel: (268) 460-9400
Fax: (268) 560-2211

Charlesworth Brown
Nevis Street
Tel: (268) 462-1012
Fax: (268) 462-2568

Charles Samuel
High Street
Tel: (268) 462-3442

Gail Christian
17 Church Street
St John's
Tel: (268) 462-0227
Fax: (268) 462-3772

Christian, Lovell Walwyn & Co
29 Redcliffe Street
St John's
Tel: (268) 462-1136
Fax: (268) 461-0767

Craig Christopher
26 Cross Street
Tel: (268) 462-0073
Fax: (268) 462-1118

Clarke & Clarke
Bishop Lodge Building
Tel: (268) 462-0732
Fax: (268) 462-0720

Commodore & Associates
26 Cross Street
Tel: (268) 462-0073
Fax: (268) 462-1118

Cort & Associates
Church Street
Tel: (268) 462-5232
Fax: (268) 462-5234
Email: cortast@candw.ag

Keith Forde & Associates
St Mary's Street
Tel: (268) 462-9030
Fax: (268) 462-9028

Patricia Forde-Simon
High Street
Tel: (268) 462-5339
Fax: (268) 462-5390

Monique Francis-Gordon
Lower St Mary's Street
Tel: (268) 562-3847
Fax: (268) 562-4337
Email: magpie@candw.ag

Nicholas Fuller
Old Parham Road
Tel: (268) 562-2413

E Ann Henry & Associates
13 Church Street
Tel: (268) 462-2127
Fax: (268) 462-2128
Email: eannhenry@candw.ag

Hill & Hill Chambers
Long Street
St John's
Tel: (268) 462-5939
Fax: (268) 462-1127
Email: hill&hill@actol.net

James & Associates
Redcliffe Street
Tel: (268) 462-1459
Fax: (268) 462-1444

Kelvin John
Lower Factory Road
Tel: (268) 460-5860
Fax: (268) 462-9114

Kelsick & Kelsick
Redcliffe Street
St John's
Tel: (268) 460-9133

Joyce Kentish
St Mary's Street
St John's
Tel: (268) 462-1012
Fax: (268) 462-2568

Lake & Kentish Chambers
St Mary's Street
Tel: (268) 462-1012
Fax: (268) 462-2568
Email: lakent@candw.ag

Bernice V Lake
St Mary's Street
Tel: (268) 462-1012
Fax: (268) 462-2568

Lockhart Mendes & Co
17 Church Street
Tel: (268) 462-0227
Fax: (268) 462-3772

Marshall & Co
#5 Redcliffe Street
St John's
Tel: (268) 462-3562
Fax: (268) 462-3563
Email: m&co@hcmlaw.com

Jason Martin
29 Redcliffe Street
Tel: (268) 462-1136
Fax: (268) 461-0767
Email: chris.co@candw.ag

Georgice Mendes-Blackman
17 Church Street
Tel: (268) 462-0227
Fax: (268) 462-3772

Sylvia O'Mard-Camacho
23 High Street
Tel: (268) 462-1679
Fax: (268) 462-8778
Email: omards@candw.ag

Septimus Rhudd
6 Temple Street
Tel: (268) 460-6184
Fax: (268) 460-6183
Email: lawrhudd@candw.ag

Richards Anjo & Associates
Lower Long Street
Tel: (268) 562-1705
Fax: (268) 562-1706

Roberts & Co
60 Nevis Street
Tel: (268) 462-0076
Fax: (268) 462-3077
Email: robertslaw@candw.ag

Simon & Associates
Newgate Street
St John's
Tel: (268) 462-4468
Fax: (268) 462-0327
Email: chancellor@candw.ag

Sydney P Christian & Associates
20 Redcliffe Street
Tel: (268) 462-1136
Fax: (268) 461-0767

LAWYERS / ATTORNEYS (Cont'd)

Arthur Thomas
Lower Factory Road
Tel: (268) 460-5860
Fax: (268) 462-9114

John Thomas
Lower Factory Road
Tel: (268) 460-5860
Fax: (268) 462-9114

Vernon Tomlinson
Redcliffe Street
St John's
Tel: (268) 462-1459
Fax: (268) 462-1444

Jacqueline Walwyn
20 Redcliffe Street
Tel: (268) 462-1136
Fax: (268) 461-0767

Wason & Wason
Redcliffe Street
St John's
Tel: (268) 462-4044
Fax: (268) 462-4044

Watt & Associates
55 Newgate Street
St John's
Tel: (268) 462-1136
Fax: (268) 462-1354

LIBRARIES

Antigua & Barbuda Public Library
Market Street
Tel: (268) 462-0229

Law Library
St Mary's & Temple Streets
Tel: (268) 462-0626

MEDIA

RADIO

ABS Radio
Old Parham Road
Tel: (268) 462-2998
Fax: (268) 562-2801
Email: absradio@ab.gov.ag

CANA News
Tel: (268) 460-2458
Fax: (268) 460-2458
Email: colo_tintin@hotmail.com

Crusader Radio
Redcliffe Street
St John's
Tel: (268) 562-4911
Fax: (268) 562-4613
Email: crusadernews@candw.ag

Family Radio
Tel: (268) 560-7578
Fax: (268) 560-7577
Email: family@caribmail.com

Gem Radio
Tel: (268) 462-6222
Fax: (268) 462-6224
Email: gemradio@candw.ag

Observer Radio 911
High Street
Tel: (268) 481-9100
Fax: (268) 481-9125
Email: voice@radio911fm.com

Sun FM/ZDK Radio
Ottos
Tel: (268) 462-1101
Fax: (268) 462-1101
Email: zdknews@hotmail.com

PRINT

Antigua Sun
Coolidge
Tel: (268) 480-5960
Fax: (268) 480-5968
Email: editor@antiguasun.com

Daily Observer
Coolidge
Tel: (268) 480-1750
Fax: (268) 480-1757
Email: dailyobserver@candw.ag

The Sunday Scoop
High Street
Tel: (268) 562-4864
Fax: (268) 562-4964
Email: thescoop@candw.ag

TELEVISION

ABS TV
Cross Street
Tel: (268) 462-1233
Fax: (268) 462-4442
Email: antiguatv@hotmail.com

CTV
Long Street
Tel: (268) 462-4224
Fax: (268) 462-4211

GIS News
Cross Street
Tel: (268) 462-2869
Fax: (268) 462-4442
Email: gisnews@hotmail.com

NIGHTCLUBS / BARS

Abracadabra Bar & Restaurant
English Harbour
Tel: (268) 460-2701

The Beach
Dickenson Bay
Tel: (268) 480-6940

Big Banana
Redcliffe Quay
St John's
Tel: (268) 480-6985

Catcus Bar & Restaurant
Falmouth
Tel: (268) 460-6575

Coconut Grove Restaurant & Beach
Bar
Dickenson Bay
Tel: (268) 462-1538

Grand Princess
Jolly Harbour
Tel: (268) 562-9900

Dogwatch Tavern
Jolly Harbour
Tel: (268) 462-6550

Joemikes Downtown Plaza
(Corner of) Nevis Street & Corn
Alley
Tel: (268) 462-1142

King's Casino
Heritage Quay
Tel: (268) 462-1727

Liquid Nightclub
2nd Floor Grand Princess
Jolly Harbour
Tel: (268) 562-7874

O'Grady's Pub
Redcliffe Street
Tel: (268) 462-5392

Rush Nightclub
Runaway Bay
Tel: (268) 562-7874

Steely Bar BBR Sportive
Jolly Harbour
Tel: (268) 462-6260

PHARMACIES

Alpha Pharmacy
Redcliffe Street
Tel: (268) 462-1112

Ceco Pharmacy
High Street
Tel: (268) 562-4706
Fax: (268) 462-0225

City Pharmacy
St Mary's Street
Tel: (268) 480-3314
Fax: (268) 480-3310

Cornerstone Pharmacy
Upper Newgate Street
Tel: (268) 462-7859

Dyett Pharmacy
Cross Street
Tel: (268) 462-0925

EVC Health & Beauty Store
Lower New Street
Tel: (268) 562-4545

Food City Pharmacy
Deep Water Harbour
Tel: (268) 462-4808
Fax: (268) 480-8729

Grace Green Pharmacy
Christian Street
Tel: (268) 463-0888

Health Pharmacy
Redcliffe Street
Tel: (268) 462-1255

Hill's Drug Mart
Long Street
Tel: (268) 460-6710

JFK Pharmacy
Long Street
Tel: (268) 562-1621

Liberty Pharmacy
Liberta Village
Tel: (268) 460-4994

Medical Benefits Scheme
Nevis Street
Tel: (268) 462-1621
Fax: (268) 462-3318

Natures Family Store (Family
Pharmacy)
Lower Market Street
Tel: (268) 462-1153
Fax: (268) 462-1153

Piper's Pharmacy
All Saints Road
Tel: (268) 462-0736
Fax: (268) 462-0736

Ramco Pharmacy
Camacho's Avenue
Tel: (268) 462-2944

Reliance Pharmacy
Redcliffe Street
Tel: (268) 462-4646
Fax: (268) 462-4874

Shopper's Pharmacy Ltd
High Street
St John's
Tel: (268) 462-4706
Fax: (268) 462-7779

Stevens Pharmacy
Temple & Redcliffe Streets
Tel: (268) 462-2214

Super Drug Store
Popeshead & Bishopgate Streets
Tel: (268) 460-5018

Sysco Pharmacy
Jolly Harbour
Tel: (268) 462-5917

Woods Pharmacy
Woods Centre
Tel: (268) 462-9287
Fax: (268) 462-9289

PHOTOGRAPHERS

Hot Shot Photo
Sandals Resort
Tel: (268) 463-8648
Fax: (268) 460-9646

Island Photo
Redcliffe Street
St John's
Tel: (268) 462-1567
Fax: (268) 462-7726

Jackal Photo Studio
Wireless Road
Tel: (268) 462-0640

Joseph Jones Photography
Ffryes Estate
Tel: (268) 462-7317
Cell: (268) 774-7317

Photo Shak Ltd
St John's
Tel: (268) 773-9084
Fax: (268) 562-1052

PHOTOGRAPHERS (Cont'd)

Skip's Photo Studio
St Mary's Street
Tel: (268) 462-5878
Fax: (268) 462-5878

Soul Train Photo Studio
Vivian Richards Street
Tel: (268) 462-0850

Tots Plus Photo Studio
Tel: (268) 462-9588
Fax: (268) 462-9588

Images.Cam Photo Studio
Redcliffe Quay
Tel: (268) 463-6099

Photogenesis Imaging
Michael's Avenue
Tel: (268) 462-1066
Fax: (268) 562-2901

POLICE

Royal Police Force of Antigua &
Barbuda (Headquarters)
American Road
Tel: (268) 462-0125/6/7
Fax: (268) 462-0954

Police Stations

All Saints
    Tel: (268) 460-6753
Bolans
    Tel: (268) 462-1080
Brooks
    Tel: (268) 463-1065
Barbuda
    Tel: (268) 460-0074
Coolidge
    Tel: (268) 462-3185
Dockyard
    Tel: (268) 460-1002
Freetown
    Tel: (268) 460-4121
Grays Farm
    Tel: (268) 462-0481
Liberta
    Tel: (268) 460-1001
Parham
    Tel: (268) 463-2060
St John's
    Tel: (268) 462-0045/6/7
Wilikies
    Tel: (268) 463-2000

POST OFFICES

General Post Office
High & Long Streets
Tel: (268) 562-1928
Fax: (268) 460-9650

Branch Post Offices

All Saints
    Tel: (268) 460-1087
Barbuda
    Tel: (268) 460-0075
Dockyard
    Tel: (268) 460-1519
V.C. Bird International Airport
    Tel: (268) 462-3221
Woods Mall
    Tel: (268) 462-9590

Sub Post Offices

Bethesda
    Tel: (268) 463-2756
Bolans
    Tel: (268) 462-0936
Cedar Grove
    Tel: (268) 461-2269
Freetown
    Tel: (268) 460-4041
Five Islands
    Tel: 461-4307
New Winthropes
    Tel: 461-5060
Old Road/Johnson Point
    Tel: (268) 462-9111
Parham
    Tel: (268) 463-3560
Seatons
    Tel: (268) 463-2288

RELIGIOUS INSTITUTIONS

All Saints Church of the Nazarene
Matthews Road
Tel: (268) 463-8710

All Saints Pentecostal
Matthews Road
Tel: (268) 460-2122

Bahai Faith
All Saints Road
Tel: (268) 461-2366

Barbuda Pentecostal Church
Codrington, Barbuda
Tel: (268) 460-0101

Barbuda Seventh Day Adventist
Church
Codrington
Tel: (268) 460-0430

Barbuda Wesleyan Holiness Church
Barbuda
Tel: (268) 460-0048

Beacon Light Church of the Nazarene
Villa
Tel: (268) 460-5958

Bethel Anglican Church
Lower St John's Street
Tel: (268) 460-5931

Bethesda Pentecostal Church
Bethesda
Tel: (268) 463-2713

Bible Believers Fellowship Ministries
Cassada Gardens
Tel: (268) 460-5923

Bolans Church of the Nazarene
Bolans
Tel: (268) 462-7762

Bolans Pentecostal Assembly
Bolans
Tel: (268) 462-7198

Caribbean Conference of Churches
Bishopgate Street
Tel: (268) 462-0261

Cathedral Parish of St John's
St John's Street
Tel: (268) 562-1800

Catholic Holy Family Cathedral
Michael's Mount
Tel: (268) 462-2410

Central Baptist Church
Radio Range
Tel: (268) 462-2894
Fax: (268) 462-6029

Christian Action for the
Development in the Caribbean
Redcliffe Street
St John's
Tel: (268) 462-0261

Christian Faith Academy
Golden Grove
Tel: (268) 560-6037
Fax: (268) 560-0398

Christian Union Mission
Clarehall
Tel: (268) 461-1905

Church of Christ
Golden Grove Main Road
Tel: (268) 461-6732

Church of God
Swetes Village
Tel: (268) 460-2390

Church of God of Prophecy
Rowan Henry Street
Gambles
Tel: (268)462-1830

Church of Jesus Christ Latter Day
Saints
Fort Road
Tel: (268) 461-2237

Deeper Life Church
Golden Grove
Tel: (268) 461-7676

English Harbour Pentecostal Church
English Harbour
Tel: (268) 460-1270

Faith & Power Ministries
Paynters Industrial Site
Tel: (268) 460-8741
Fax: (268) 460-8742

Gilbert Ecumenical Centre
Mercers Creek
Tel: (268) 463-2519

Grace Baptist Church
Gambles Terrace
Tel: (268) 462-4230

Grays Farm Seventh Day Adventist
Church
Grays Farm
Tel: (268) 463-8015

Holiness Temple Church
Tindale Road
Tel: (268) 462-2969

Hoy Trinity Rectory
Barbuda
Tel: (268) 460-0010

Jennings New Testament Church
Jennings
Tel: (268) 462-6228

Jesus is the Answer
Paynters
Tel: (268) 460-1579

Kentish Pentecostal Church
Whenner Road
Tel: (268) 462-0752

Kingdom Hall of Jehovah Witness
Gambles Terrace
Tel: (268) 463-6295

Kiwanis Prayer Hotline
Tel: (268) 562-7729

Leeward Island Baptist Mission
Crosbies
Tel: (268) 461-2902

Liberta Seventh Day Adventist
Church
Liberta Village
Tel: (268) 460-1086

Living Faith BAptiste Church
Codrington Barbuda
Tel: (268) 460-0447

Lutheran St John's Ev Church
Radio Range
Tel: (268) 462-2896

Maranatha Baptist Church
Jennings Village
Tel: (268) 462-7130

Moravian Churches

Cana, Swetes Village
    Tel: (268) 460-1012
Cedar Hall, Jennings
    Tel: (268) 462-4330
Spring Gardens, St John's Street
    Tel: (268) 461-0656
Lebanon, Seaview Farm
    Tel: (268) 463-1007
Grace Bay, Johnson's Point
    Tel: (268) 462-8248
Gracefield, Belle View Heights
    Tel: (268) 462-6451
Cashew Hill - Tel: (268) 463-9184
Potters - Tel: (268) 460-9705
Urlings - Tel: (268)560-6788

Mount Zion Baptiste Church
Golden Grove
Tel: (268) 462-8700

New Testament Church
Bendals
Tel: (268) 462-5925

New Testament Church of God
Brownes Avenue
Tel: (268) 461-7357

New Winthropes Wesleyan Holiness
Chuch
New Winthropes
Tel: (268) 463-4386

Olivet Pentecostal Church
Liberta
Tel: (268) 460-3272

Our Lady of the Valley Anglican
Church
The Valley
Tel: (268) 462-7318

RELIGIOUS INSTITUTIONS (Cont'd)

Pares Pentecostal Church
Pares Village
Tel: (268) 463-2222

Pigotts Pentecostal Church
Fitches Creek
Tel: (268) 463-8314

Potters Pentecostal Church
Potters Village
Tel: (268) 461-9208

St Andrew's Anglican Church
Fort Road
Tel: (268) 462-4026

St Boniface Church
Martins Village
Tel: (268) 461-1742

St Georges Rectory
Judges Hill
Tel: (268) 461-3154

St John's Cathedral
Newgate Street
Tel: (268) 462-4686

St John's Pentecostal Church
Bishopgate Street
St John's
Tel: (268) 461-1146

St Paul's Anglican Rectory
Falmouth
Tel: (268) 460-1089

St Stephens Anglican Rectory
Glanvilles
Tel: (268) 463-2034

Salvation Army Church
Long Street
St John's
Tel: (268) 462-0115
Fax: (268) 462-9134

Seventh Day Adventist Churches

Old Road
    Tel: (268) 462-8623
Bendals Village
    Tel: 463-4205
Liberta
    Tel: (268) 460-1086
Nevis Street
    Tel: (268) 462-3307
Redcliffe Street
    Tel: 462-6067
Potters
    Tel: (268)560-2024
Seaglans, Glanvilles
    Tel: (268) 560-2979

Shilo Gospel Hall
Nevis Street
Tel: (268) 462-3299

Tyrells Baptist Church
Liberta
Tel: (268) 460-3557

Villa Baptist Church
Amy Byer Street
Tel: (268) 461-7773

Wesleyan Holiness Church
Parham
Tel: (268) 463-2163

Wesleyan Holiness Church
Barbuda
Tel: (268) 460-0048

Zion Church of God

North Street
    Tel: (268) 463-4149
Bendals
    Tel: (268) 461-6787
Bethesda
    Tel: 463-2776
Freemansville
    Tel: (268) 461-6702
Seaview Farm
    Tel: (268) 461-1933

RESTAURANTS

Abracadraba Restaurant
English Harbour
Tel: (268) 460-1732

Admirals Inn
Nelsons Dockyard
Tel: (268) 460-1027

Al Porto Restaurant
Jolly Harbour
Tel: (268) 462-7695

Alberto's Restaurant
Willoughby Bay
Tel: (268) 460-3007
Fax: (268) 460-3007

Amigo's Mexican Restaurant
Runaway Bay
Tel: (268) 562-1545
Fax: (268) 461-3304

Barry's Café & Bakery
Long Street
Tel: (268) 562-4310

Bayhouse Restaurant
Tradewinds Hotel
Tel: (268) 462-1223
Fax: (268) 462-5007

Bellyful
Lower All Saints Road
Tel: (268) 562-4098
Fax: (268) 562-4099

Best Health Vegetarian Restaurant
Airport Road
Tel: (268) 462-1933

Big Banana Holding Co (Pizzas)
Redcliffe Quay
Tel: (268) 480-6985
Fax (268) 480-6989

Big Banana 1761 (Airport Restaurant)
V C Bird International Airport
Tel: (268) 480-6979
Fax: (268) 480-6999

Blue Waters Beach Hotel
Blue Waters
Tel: (268) 462-0290
Fax: (268) 462-0293

Boardwalk Bar & Grill
Heritage Quay
St John's
Tel: (268) 562-3231
Fax: (268) 562-3233

Bocciolo Italian Restaurant
Jolly Beach Resort
Tel: (268) 462-0061
Fax: (268) 562-2302

Calypso Restaurant
Airport Road
Tel: (268)562-3067

Cap Horn Restaurant & Pizza
English Harbour
Tel: (268) 460-1194

Caribbean Taste Restaurant
English Harbour
Tel: (268)562-3049

Catherine's Café
English Harbour
Tel: (268) 460-5050

Charissma
St John's Street
St John's
Tel: (268) 562-2228

City View Hotel & Restaurant
Newgate Street
St John's
Tel: (268) 562-1211
Fax: (268) 562-0242

Claudia's Place
Long Street
Tel: (268) 562-1060

Coconut Grove Restaurant & Beach Bar
Dickenson Bay
Tel: (268) 462-1538
Fax: (268) 462-2162

Cocos Hotel & Restaurant
Valley Road
Tel: (268) 462-9700
Fax: (268) 462-9423

Colombo's Italian Restaurant
Galleon Beach
Tel: (268) 460-1452
Fax: (2680 460-1450

Commissioner Grill
Redcliffe Street
Tel: (268) 462-1883
Fax: (268) 462-1856

Creole Beach Bar Restaurant
Crabbe Hill
Tel: (268) 562-2218

Curry House
Redcliffe Quay
Tel: (268) 462-1895

Delightful Chinese Restaurant
Upper St Mary's Street
Tel: (268) 462-5780
Fax: (268) 562-4286

Downtown Food Mall
(Corner of) High & Market Streets
Tel: (268) 460-8474

Famous Mauros Bar & Restaurant Pizzeria
English Harbour
Tel: (268) 460-1318

Fojee's Restaurant
All Saints Road
Tel: (268) 462-2406

Galley Restaurant
Nelson's Dockyard
Tel: (268) 460-1533

Grace Before Meals
English Harbour
Tel: (268) 460-1298

HQ Restaurant & Bar
Nelson's Dockyard
Tel: (268) 562-2563

Harbour Café
Jolly Harbour
Tel: (268) 462-6026

Hemmingway's Caribbean Café
St Mary's Street
St John's
Tel: (268) 462-2763

Hemispheres International Restaurant
Jolly Beach Resort
Tel: (268) 462-0061
Fax: (268) 562-2302

Home Restaurant
Gambles
Tel: (268) 461-7651
Fax: (268) 461-0277

Jazzie'z
Valley Church Beach
Tel: (268) 560-2582
Fax: (268) 560-5182

Jimmy's
Catamaran, Falmouth
Tel: (268) 463-8866

Joe Mike's Hotel Plaza
Nevis Street
Tel: (268) 462-1142
Fax: (268) 462-6056
E: mail: joemikes@candw.ag

Julian's Alfresco
Barrymore Beach Club
Runaway Bay
Tel: (268) 562-1545
Tel: (268) 460-1662

Kentucky Fried Chicken (KFC) Ltd
High Street & Fort Road
Tel: (268) 462-1951 / 9415
Fax: (268) 462-3485

La Perruche Restaurant
English Harbour
Tel: (268) 460-3040

Last Lemmins Bar & Restaurant
Falmouth Harbour
Tel: (268) 460-6910

Le Cap Horn
English Harbour
Tel: (268) 460-1194
Fax: (268) 460-1793

RESTAURANTS (Cont'd)

Le Bistro French Restaurant
Hodges Bay
Tel: (268) 462-3881
Fax: (268) 461-2996
Email: pgbistro@candw.ag

Lobster Pot
Runaway Bay
Tel: (268) 462-2855
Fax: (268) 462-7966

Lord Nelson Beach Hotel
Dutchman's Bay, Coolidge
Tel: (268) 462-3094
Fax: (268) 462-3094

Lydia's Caribbean Seafood
Restaurant
Jolly Beach Hotel
Tel: (268) 462-0061
Fax: (268) 562-2302

Mama Lolly's Vegetarian Café
Redcliffe Quay
Tel: (268) 562-1552
Fax: (268) 562-1552

Melini's Ristorante/Pizzeria
Jolly Harbour
Tel: (268) 562-4173
Fax: (268) 560-8952

Mid East Fast Food
Upper Newgate Street & Redcliffe
Quay
Tel: (268) 562-0101 / 3663
Fax: (268) 560-9595

Miller's By the Sea
Fort James
Tel: (268) 462-9414
Fax: (268) 462-9591

Natural N'yam Vegetarian
Restaurant
Cross Street
Tel: (268) 562-0174

New Thriving Chinese Restaurant
Long Street/Airport Road
Tel: (268) 462-4611 / 562-0046

O J's Bar & Restaurant
Crabbe Hill
Tel: (268) 460-0184

O'Grady's Pub
Redcliffe Street
St John's
Tel: (268) 462-5392

Palm Tree Restaurant
Barbuda
Tel: (268) 460-0517

Papa Zouk Fish & Rum
Upper Gambles
Tel: (268) 464-7576 / 6044

Pari's Pizza & Steakhouse
Tradewinds
Tel: (268) 462-1501
Fax: (268) 461-1508

Peter's BBQ & Steakhouse
Jolly Harbour
Tel: (268) 462-6026

Philtons Bakery Café
Friars Hill Road
Tel: (268) 463-2253

Pita Pocket & Snack
Nevis Street
Tel: (268) 562-4136
Fax: (268) 463-6885

Rainbow's End Restaurant
Bolans Village
Tel: (268) 562-2789

Red Octopus Seafood Restaurant
English Harbour
Tel: (268) 460-1882

Roti King
St Mary's Street
Tel: (268) 462-2328

Russell's Bar & Seafood Restaurant
Fort James
Tel: (268) 462-5479

Sea Breeze Café
Antigua Yacht Club
Tel: (268) 562-3739

Sheer at Cocobay Resort
Cocobay Resort
Tel: (268) 562-2400
Fax: (268) 562-2424

Shirley Heights Lookout
Shirley Heights
Tel: (268) 460-1785

Skulduggery Café
Antigua Yacht Club Marina
Tel: (268) 460-1444

Southern Cross Restaurant
Yacht Club
Tel: (268) 460-1797
Fax: (268) 460-1797

Southern Fry Restaurant
Lower Market Street & Old Parham Rd
Tel: (268) 462-1616

Spliff Bar & Grill
Old Parham Road
Tel: (268) 463-8611
Fax: (268) 562-4553

Steely Bar & Restaurant at BBR
Sportive
Jolly Harbour
Tel: (268) 462-6260
Fax: (268) 460-8182

Sticky Wicket Restaurant & Bar
Coolidge
Tel: (268) 481-7000
Fax: (268) 481-7010

The Beach
Dickenson Bay
Tel: (268) 480-6940
Fax: (268) 480-6943

The Beach House
Barbuda
Tel: (268) 764-4203

The Cappuccino Lounge
Nelson's Alley
Tel: (268) 562-6808

The Docksider
St James's Club
Tel: (268) 460-5000

The Green Door Tavern
Madison's Square, Barbuda
Tel: (268) 562-3134

The Palm Restaurant
Blue Waters Hotel
Tel: (268) 462-0290

The Pavillion
Coolidge
Tel: (268) 481-6800

The Pitch Bar & Restaurant
Coolidge
Tel: (268) 461-1417 / 462-1417

The Shell Beach Pub
Coolidge
Tel: (268) 461-1417
Tel: (268) 462-1417

The Terrace Restaurant
The Inn at English Harbour
Tel: (268) 460-1014

The Verandah Bar
Jumby Bay Resort
Tel: (268) 462-6000

Three Martini Beach Bar Restaurant
& Apartments
Crabbe Hill
Tel: (268) 480-9306
Fax: (268) 481-1735

The Terrace Restaurant
Inn at English Harbour
Tel: (268) 460-1014

Turner's Beach Bar & Restaurant
Johnson's Point
Tel: (268) 462-9133
Fax: (268) 560-8114

Trappas Bar
Dockyard Drive
Tel: (268) 562-3534

Ustav
Jolly Beach Hotel
Tel: (268) 462-0061
Fax: (268) 562-2302

Vyvien's
Blue Waters Hotel
Tel: (268) 462-0290

Warri Pier Restaurant
Rex Halcyon Cove
Tel: (268) 462-0256
Fax: (268) 462-0271

SCUBA DIVING & WATERSPORTS

Adventure Antigua
Tel: (268) 727-3261

Antigua Seafaris
Tel: (268) 464-3571

Deep Bay Divers
Redcliffe Quay
Tel: (268) 463-8000
Fax: (268) 463-8000

Dockyard Divers
Nelson's Dockyard
Tel: (268) 460-1178
Fax: (268) 460-5850

Dolphin Fantaseas
Tel: (268) 562-7946

H 2 O Antigua Beach Club
Dutchman's Bay
Tel: (268) 562-3933

Island Speedboats Ltd
Jolly Harbour
Tel: (268) 774-1810

Jolly Harbour Watersports
Jolly Harbour
Tel: (268) 462-7979 / 774-3005

Kite Antigua
Jabberwok Beach
Tel: (268) 727-3983

Long Bay Hotel
Long Bay
Tel: (268) 463-2005

Missa Ferdie
Tel: (268) 462-1440 / 460-1503

Nightwing
Tel: (268) 464-4665

Obsession Deep Sea Fishing Charters
Hodges Bay
Tel: (268) 462-2824
Fax: (268) 462-3496

Overdraft
Tel: (268) 462-1961 / 464-4954

Paddles Kayak Eco Trips
Seaton's Village
Tel: (268) 463-1944
Fax: (268) 463-3344

Sandals
Dickenson Bay
Tel: (268) 462-0267

SeaSports
Dickenson Bay
Tel: (268) 462-3355
Fax: (268) 463-0722

Shore Tours Antigua
Dickenson Bay
Tel: (268) 462-6326

Stingray City Antigua Ltd
Seaton's Village
Tel: (268) 562-7297
Fax: (268) 562-7297

Sunsail Club Colonna
Hodges Bay
Tel: (268) 462-6263

SCHOOLS

Secondary

All Saints Secondary School
Tel: (268) 460-1009

Antigua Girls High School
Tel: (268) 462-0404

Antigua Grammar School
Tel: (268) 462-1050

Christ the King High School
Tel: (268) 462-0570

Holy Trinity School
Barbuda
Tel: (268) 460-0095

Jennings Secondary
Tel: (268) 462-0106

Ottos Comprehensive School
Tel: (268) 462-3570

Pares Secondary School
Tel: (268) 463-2045

Princess Margaret School
Tel: (268) 462-0422

St Joseph's Academy
Tel: (268) 462-2121

Primary

Baptist Academy of Antigua
Tel: (268) 462-2894

Bendals Primary School
Tel: (268) 462-6944

Bethesda Primary School
Tel: (268) 463-2777

Bolans Primary School
Tel: (268) 462-7400

Buckley's Primary School
Tel: (268) 460-2485

Cedar Grove Primary School
Tel: (268) 462-0221

Clare Hall Secondary School
Tel: (268) 462-3487

Cobbs Cross Primary School
Tel: (268) 460-3401

Five Islands Primary School
Tel: (268) 462-6173

Foundation Mixed School
Tel: (268) 462-0672

Freetown Primary School
Tel: (268) 460-4332

Glanvilles Primary School
Tel: (268) 463-3466

Golden Grove Primary School
Tel: (268) 462-1267

Grace Christian Academy
Tel: (268) 462-4242

Green Bay Primary School
Tel: (268) 462-4495

Greensville Primary School
Tel: (268) 562-3383

Holy Trinity School
Barbuda
Tel: (268) 460-0095

Irene Williams Primary School
Tel: (268) 460-3757

J T Ambrose Primary School
Tel: (268) 460-2272

Jennings Primary School
Tel: (268) 460-6070

John Hughes Primary School
Tel: (268) 460-3999

Liberta Primary School
Tel: (268) 460-3444

Lutheran Primary School
Tel: (268) 462-2896

Mary E. Pigott Primary School
Tel: (268) 462-2004

Newfield Primary School
Tel: (268) 460-4320

New Winthropes Primary School
Tel: (268) 462-2984

Old Road Primary School
Tel: (268) 462-8421

Pares Primary School
Tel: (268) 463-6078

Parham Primary School
Tel: (268) 463-3660

Potters Primary School
Tel: (268) 462-6204

Sea View Farm Primary School
Tel: (268) 463-2931

St John's Catholic Primary
Tel: (268) 462-0113

St Michael's School
Tel: (268) 462-4805

St Nicholas Primary School
Tel: (268) 462-0831

Sunnydale School
Tel: (268) 462-1347

Sunnyside Tutorial School
Tel: (268) 462-1495

T N Kirnon Primary School
Tel: (268) 462-4267

TOR Memorial High School
Tel: (268) 460-7101

SERVICE STATIONS

ACE Enterprises Ltd
Factory Road
Tel: (268) 462-1289

Chandler's Service Station
Cross Street
Tel: (268) 462-1342

Collins Pumping Station
Tel: (268) 463-2023

Eastside Service Station
Glanvilles
Tel: (268) 462-4047

Ebenezer Service Station
Ebenezer Village
Tel: (268) 462-7497

Frankie's Service Station
Lyons Estate
Tel: (268) 463-4122

Friars Hill Service Station
Friars Hill Road
Tel: (268) 462-3285

G E T Enterprises
(Corner of) Factory Road & Queen
Elizabeth Highway
Tel: (268) 462-1898

Golden Grove Service Station
Golden Grove Main Road
Tel: (268) 462-9179

James Service Centre
Deep Water Harbour
Tel: (268) 462-2364

M & M Accessories Plus
Old Parham Road
Tel: (268) 481-5000

Midway Service Station
Clarks Hill
Tel: (268) 463-1035

Percival's Enterprises Ltd
Fort Road
Tel: (268) 462-1464

Robinson's Service Station
All Saints Road
Tel: (268) 462-0484

WIOC Service Station
Airport Road
Tel: (268) 462-3194

Spencer's Servicentre
Factory Road
Tel: (268) 462-2154

Valley Road Service Station
Valley Road
Tel: (268) 462-0425

SHIPPING

Bryson's Shipping Agency
Tel: (268) 480-1240
Fax: (268) 462-0170

Caribbean Forwarders Co Ltd
Friars Hill Road
Tel: (268) 480-1100

Caribbean Maritime Services Ltd
Scotts Hill
Tel: (268) 462-1224
Fax: (268) 462-1227
Email: caribms@candw.ag

Caribseas Ltd
North Street & Wapping Lane
Tel: (268) 462-4863
Fax: (268) 462-4864
Email: caribsea@candw.ag

Vernon G Edwards
(Corner of) Thames & Long Streets
Tel: (268) 462-2034
Fax: (268) 462-2035

Francis Trading Agency Ltd
High Street
Tel: (268) 462-4555
Fax: (268) 462-0849
Email: fta@candw.ag

Inter-Freight Ltd
Lower Bishopgate Street
Tel: (268) 481-1200
Fax: (268) 481-1216
Email: ifreight@candw.ag

Inter-Island Sales & Supply
Newgate Street
St John's
Tel: (268) 481-1211
Fax: (268) 481-1212

International Shipping & Trading
Co Ltd
Tel: (268) 462-5612
Fax: (268) 462-5611

Jasco Agencies Ltd
St John's Street
St John's
Tel: (268) 462-9521
Fax: (268) 462-9524

Walker's Trading Agency
North Street
Tel: (268) 462-4121
Fax: (268) 462-4122

SUPERMARKETS

Bailey's C E Supermarket
Falmouth
Tel: (268) 460-1142

Bargain Centre Supermarket Ltd
Perry Bay
Tel: (268) 481-4493

Benjie's Supermarket
Sea View Farm
Tel: (268) 463-1101

Billy's Food Mart
Friars Hill Road
Tel: (268) 480-2015

Burton's Grocery
Barbuda
Tel: (268) 460-0607

Christo's Supermarket
High Street, Old Parham Road &
Fort Road
Tel: (268) 462-1073/0719
Tel: (268) 460-6678

Da Silva Grocery
St Johnson's Village
Tel: (268) 560-0246

Destin's Supermarket
(Corner of) North Street & Wilkinson
Cross
Tel: (268) 462-1166

Dockside Liquors & Supermarket
Antigua Yacht Club Marina
Tel: (268) 463-9000

Eileen Supermarket
Golden Grove
Tel: (268) 562-2834

SUPERMARKETS (Cont'd)

The Epicurean
Friars Hill Road & Jolly Harbour
Complex
Tel: (268) 462-2565
Tel: (268) 462-7705

Food Brokerages Services Ltd
Upper Newgate Street & South
Street
St John's
Tel: (268) 480-2010
Tel: (268) 480-2000

Food City
Harbour Road
Tel: (268) 480-8720

Food Emporium
Long & Church Streets
Tel: (268) 480-8710

Gloria Ltd
Whenner Road
Tel: (268) 462-4100

Gourmet Basket
Airport Road
Tel: (268) 480-5174

Grant Brothers Supermarket
Perry Bay
Tel: (268) 462-4954

H & H Supermarket
#2 Cassada Gardens
Tel: (268) 461-9604

La Suprette
Wilikies Village
Tel: (268) 463-3459

Market Point Supermarket
Market Street
St John's
Tel: (268) 462-6317

Nearby Supermarket
Ottos Main Road
Tel: (268) 462-0689

Northshore Supermarket
Cedar Grove
Tel: (268) 462-0098

O'Beez Food Store & Wholesale
Factory Road
Tel: (268) 462-4660

Pond View Superette
Old Road
Tel: (268) 462-8617

Price Rite Supermarket
Glanvilles Village
Tel: (268) 463-4018

Sammy Superette & Self Service
All Saints Road
Tel: (268) 462-2195

Sheila Supermarket
Pigotts Village
Tel: (268) 463-8040

Shop Smart Superette
Armstrong Road
Tel: (268) 463-6385

Silver Lining Supermarket
Ottos Main Road
Tel: (268) 462-3721

Supermarket Espanol
Lower All Saints Road
Tel: (268) 562-2497

Walker Supermarket
Golden Grove
Tel: (268) 462-1568

Walt's Supermarket
Old Parham Road
Tel: (268) 462-5496

Wheels Supermarket
Wireless Road
Tel: (268) 461-1945

Galstron's
Old Parham Road
Tel: (268) 462-9509

TAXI SERVICES

Antigua Reliable 24hr Taxi Service
West Bus Station
Tel: (268) 460-5353

Archibald Taxi Service
Powells
Tel: (268) 562-1709

Brother's Taxi Service
Lower Long Street
Tel: (268) 462-6464

Christo Taxi Stand
High Street
Tel: (268) 460-7434

Co-operative Taxi Service
Villa
Tel: (268) 462-4325

Daylight Taxi Service
Long Street
Tel: (268) 462-3015

Gravy Taxi Stand
Market Street
Tel: (268) 462-0711

Heritage Quay Taxi Stand
Heritage Quay
Tel: (268) 460-8213

Life Saver Taxi Stand
Lower Tanner Street
Tel: (268) 460-9898

Matthew Car Rental & Taxi Service
Tel: (268) 462-8803

Reliable Taxi Service
Fax: (268) 463-3955

Sandals Antigua Taxi Stand
Dickenson Bay
Tel: (268) 462-2504

United Taxi Association
V.C. Bird International Airport
Tel: (268) 562-0262

West Bus Station Taxi Service
Tel: (268) 462-5190

TELECOMMUNICATIONS COMPANIES

Antigua Public Utilities Authority
Cassada Gardens
Tel: (268) 480-7000
Email: apuaops@candw.ag

Cable & Wireless (WI) Ltd
Clare Hall
Tel: (268) 480-4000
Fax: (268) 480-4105

TELECOMMUNICATIONS EQUIPMENT SERVICES

The Signal Locker
Nelson's Dockyard
Tel: (268) 460-1528
Fax: (268) 460-1148

TOURIST OFFICES & OVERSEAS MISSIONS

TOURIST OFFICES

Antigua

Ministry of Tourism & Aviation
Government Complex
Queen Elizabeth Highway
P.O. Box 363
Tel: (268) 462-0480
Fax: (268) 462-2483
Email: deptourism@antigua.gov.ag

United States

Antigua and Barbuda Department of
Tourism and Trade
25 S.E. 2nd Avenue, Suite 300
Miami, FL 33131
Tel: 305-381-6762
Fax: 305-381-7908
Email: cganuear@bellsouth.net

Antigua and Barbuda Department of
Tourism and Trade
610 Fifth Avenue
Suite 311
New York, NY 10020
Tel: 212-541-4117
Fax: 212-757-1607
Email: info@antigua-barbuda.org

Canada

Antigua and Barbuda Department of
Tourism and Trade
60 St Clair Avenue East
Suite 304
Toronto, Ontario M4T 1N5
Tel: 416-961-3085
Fax: 416-961-7218
Email:
info@antigua-barbuda-ca.com

United Kingdom

Antigua and Barbuda Department of
Tourism
Antigua House
15 Thayer Street
London W1M 5LD
Tel: 44-207-486-7073/4/5
Fax: 44-207-486-9970
Email: antbar@msn.com

Germany, Australia, Switzerland, Italy & Northern Europe

Antigua & Department of Tourism
Thomasstr. 11
D 61348 – Bad Homburg, Germany
Tel: 49-6172-21504
Fax: 49-6172-21513
Email: antigua-barbuda@karibik.org

Italy

Antigua and Barbuda Department of
Tourism
Via S. Maria Alla Porta 9 20123, Milan
Tel: 03-92-87-79-83
Fax: 03-92-87-79-83
Email:
infoantigua@antigua-barbuda.org

France

Office du Tourisme D'Antigua and
Barbuda
43 Avenue Freidland, Paris 75008
Tel: 053-75-15-71
Fax: 053-75-15-69
Email:
ot.antigua-barbuda@wanadoo.fr

EMBASSIES & CONSULATES
OVERSEAS

Canada

Consulate General of Antigua and
Barbuda
60 St Clair Avenue East, Suite 304
Toronto, Ontario M4T 1N5
T: 416-961-3085. F: 416-961-7218

United Kingdom

High Commission for Antigua and
Barbuda
Antigua House, 15 Thayer Street
London W1M 5LD
Tel: 44-207-486-7073/4/5
Fax: 44-207-486-9970

United States

Embassy of Antigua and Barbuda
3216 New Mexico Avenue, N.W.
Washington, DC 20016
Tel: 202-362-5122
Fax: 202-362-5225

Permanent Mission of Antigua &
Barbuda to the United Nations
610 Fifth Avenue, Suite 311
New York, NY 10020
T: 212-541-4117. F: 212-757-1607

Consulate General of Antigua and
Barbuda
25 S.E. 2nd Avenue, Suite 300
Miami, FL 33131
T: 305-381-6762. F: 305-381-7908

People's Republic of China

Embassy of Antigua and Barbuda
People's Republic of China
Room No1N, Guomen Building No.
1, Zuojiazhuang, Chaoyang District,
Beijing 100028
Tel: 86-106-460-6481
Fax: 86-106-460-6356

TOURS & ATTRACTIONS

Cades Bay Pineapple Station
Old Road

Cenotaph
High Street

Betty's Hope Estate
Pares Village
Tel: (268) 462-4930 / 1469

Fort Barrington
Deep Bay

Fort Berkley
English Harbour
Tel: (268) 460-1379

Fort George
Monk's Hill
Tel: (268) 460-1379

Government House/Governor
General's Residence
Independence Drive
Tel: (268) 462-0003

Industrial School for the Blind
All Saints Road
Tel: (268) 462-0663

Museum of Antigua and Barbuda
Long Street
St John's
Tel: (268) 462-4930 / 1469

National Archives
Factory Road
Tel: (268) 462-3946/7

Nelson's Dockyard
English Harbour
Tel: (268) 460-1379

St John's Cathedral
Newgate & Long Streets

Westerby Memorial
High Street

Harmony Hall
Brown's Bay
Tel: (268) 460-4120

Indian Town & Devil's Bridge
East Coast

TOUR OPERATORS

Alexander Parrish (Antigua) Ltd
Thames Street
Tel: (268) 462-0187
Fax: (268) 462-4457

Antigua Vacations Ltd
Jardines Court
Tel: (268) 460-7383
Fax: (268) 4463-8959

Bo Tours
Tel: (268) 462-6632
Fax: (268) 462-5336

Coral Island Tours
Redcliffe Quay
Tel: (268) 460-5625
Fax: (268) 460-5626

Destination Antigua
Tel: (268) 463-1944
Fax: (268) 463-3344

Global Travel & Tours
High Street
Tel: (268) 480-1230
Fax: (268) 462-0320

International Travel Consultants
(ITC) Ltd
Thames & Church Street
Tel: (268) 462-0811
Fax: (268) 462-4156

National Tours
Tel: (268) 462-7979
Fax: (268) 462-7979

Nicholson's Travel Agency
English Harbour
Tel: (268) 463-7391/2
Fax: (268) 462-4802

Paradise Island Tours
Tel: (268) 462-7208
Tel: (268) 727-5632

SunTours
(Corner of) Long & Thames Street
Tel: (268) 462-4788
Fax: (268) 462-4799

Wadadli Travel & ToursLtd.
Tel: (268) 462-2227/28
Fax: (268) 462-4489

TRAVEL AGENCIES

Alexander Parrish (Antigua) Ltd
Thames Street
St John's
Tel: (268) 462-0187
Fax: (268) 462-4457

Carib World Travel
Woods Centre
Tel: (268) 480-2999
Fax: (268) 480-2985

Global Travel & Tours
High Street
St John's
Tel: (268) 480-1230
Fax: (268) 462-0320

Going Places Travel
Long & Thames Street
St John's
Tel: (268) 480-1230
Fax: (268) 462-5324

International Travel Consultants
(ITC) Ltd
Thames & Church Street
St John's
Tel: (268) 462-0811
Fax: (268) 462-4156

Nicholson's Travel Agency
English Harbour
Tel: (268) 463-7391/2
Fax: (268) 462-4802

Novella's Travel & Tours
Yacht Club Marina
Tel: (268) 460-1209
Fax: (268) 462-3352

Travel Connections Ltd
Cobbs Cross
Tel: (268) 462-3963
Fax: (268) 462-4780

Tri Star Travel Ltd
Old Parham Road
St John's
Tel: (268) 481-1702
Fax: (268) 481-1701

Wadadli Travel & ToursLtd
Tel: (268) 462-2227
Tel: (268) 462-2228
Fax: (268) 462-4489

West Indian International Tours
Briggins Road
St John's
Tel: (268) 462-0582
Fax: (268) 462-4802

WEDDING PLANNERS

Admirals Inn
Nelson's Dockyard
Tel: (268) 460-1027
Fax: (268) 460-1534
Email: admirals@candw.ag

Allegro Resort
Pineapple Beach
Tel: (268) 463-2006
Fax: (268) 463-2452
Email: info@antigua.allegroresorts

Antigua Beachcomber Hotel
Winthropes Bay
Tel: (268) 462-3100
Fax: (268) 462-4012
Email: beachcom@candw.ag

Antigua Village Condo Beach Resort
Dickenson Bay
Tel: (268) 462-2930
Fax: (268) 462-0375
Email: antiguavillage@candw.ag

Blue Waters Antigua
Blue Waters
Tel: (268) 462-0290
Fax: (268) 462-0293
Email: bluewaters@candw.ag

Cocobay Resort
Valley Church
Tel: (268) 562-2400
Fax: (268) 562-2424
Email: cocobay@candw.ag

Coco Point Lodge
Codrington
Barbuda
Tel: (268) 462-3816
Fax: (268) 462-5340

Curtain Bluff Hotel
Old Road
Tel: (268) 462-8400
Fax: (268) 462-8409
Email: curtainbluff@candw.ag

Galleon Beach Club
English Harbour
Tel: (268) 460-1024
Fax: (268) 460-1450
Email: galleonbeach@candw.ag

Galley Bay Resort
Five Islands
Tel: (268) 462-0302
Fax: (268) 462-4551
Email:
reservations@antigua-resorts.com

Hawksbill Beach Resort
Five Islands
Tel: (268) 462-0301
Fax: (268) 462-1515
Email: hawksbill@candw.ag

Jolly Beach Resort
Bolans Village
Tel: (268) 462-0061
Fax: (268) 562-2302
Email: info@jollybeachresort.com

Jumby Bay Resort
Jumby Bay Island
Tel: (268) 462-6000
Fax: (268) 462-6020
Email: jumby@candw.ag

K Club
Barbuda
Tel: (268) 460-0300
Fax: (268) 460-0305
Email: kclubbarbuda@candw.ag

Long Bay Hotel
Long Bay
Tel: (268) 463-2005
Fax: (268) 463-2439
Email: longbay@candw.ag

Rex Blue Heron
Johnsons Point
Tel: (268) 462-8564
Fax: (268) 462-8005

Rex Halcyon Cove
Dickenson Bay
Tel: (268) 462-0256
Fax: (268) 462-0271
Email: rexhalcyon@candw.ag

Sandals Antigua Resort & Spa
Dickenson Bay
Tel: (268) 462-0267
Fax: (268) 462-4135
Email: sandals@candw.ag

Siboney Beach Club
Dickenson Bay
Tel: (268) 462-0806
Fax: (268) 462-3356
Email: siboney@candw.ag

St James's Club
Mamora Bay
Tel: (268) 460-0500
Fax: (268) 460-3015
Email:
reservations@antigua-resorts.com

The Inn at English Harbour
English Harbour
Tel: (268) 460-1014
Fax: (268) 460-1603
Email: theinn@candw.ag

WEDDING SUPPLIES & SERVICES

ATS Car Rental & Limousine
Service
Powell's
Tel: (268) 562-1709
Fax: (268) 461-5700
Email: ats@candw.ag

E & G Bridal
Independence Drive
Tel: (268) 462-4002
Fax: (268) 462-5344

Occasions Party Rentals
Lyon's Estate
Tel: (268) 463-8389
Fax: (268) 460-8770

YACHT SALES & SERVICES

Antigua Slipway
English Harbour
Tel: (268) 460-10556
Fax: (268) 460-1566

Caribbean Connections
Antigua Yacht Club Marina
Tel: (268) 460-2825
Fax: (268) 460-2826

Hinkley Antigua Yacht Service
English Harbour
Tel: (268) 460-2711
Fax: (268) 460-3740

National Parks Authority
Nelson's Dockyard
Tel: (268) 481-5022
Fax: (268) 481-5047
Email: natperk@candw.ag

Nicholson Caribbean Yacht Sales
Falmouth
Tel: (268) 460-1093
Fax: (268) 460-1524

YACHT SUPPLIES & REPAIR

Antigua Rigging Ltd
Falmouth Harbour
Tel: (268) 562-2651
Fax: (268) 463-8575

Chippy/Seaward Sales
Cobbs Cross
Tel: (268) 460-1832
Fax: (268) 460-1491

YACHTS – RENTAL & CHARTER

Nicholsons Yachts Worldwide
English Harbour
Tel: (268) 460-1530
Fax: (268) 460-1531

Sunsail
Nelson's Dockyard
Tel: (268) 463-6224
Fax: (268) 460-2616
Email: charterservices@candw.ag